create jewelry
glass

create **jewelry**
glass

Brilliant Designs to Make and Wear

Marlene Blessing and Jamie Hogsett

INTERWEAVE
interweavebooks.com

For Constance, Andrea, Maggie, Valerie, and Deb—friends forever. —*MB*
For Rebecca Campbell, Laura Levaas, and Dustin Wedekind, who always have my back. —*JH*

All designs and instructions, Jamie Hogsett.
All narrative text, Marlene Blessing.
Phiotography, Joe Coca (unless otherwise specified).

Interweave Press LLC
201 East Fourth Street
Loveland, Colorado 80537 USA
interweavebooks.com

Printed in China by Asia Pacific Offset.

Library of Congress Cataloging-in-Publication Data

Blessing, Marlene, 1947-
  Create jewelry : glass : brilliant designs to make and wear / Marlene
Blessing, Jamie Hogsett, authors.
     p. cm.
  Includes index.
  ISBN 978-1-59668-067-8
 1. Jewelry making. 2. Glass beads. I. Hogsett, Jamie, 1978- II. Title.
III. Title: Glass.
  TT212.B557 2009
  739.27--dc22

                              2008038788

10 9 8 7 6 5 4 3 2 1

create **jewelry**
glass

Beauty Formed by Fire, 8

The Many Facets of Glass, 10

Glass
Beauty Formed by Fire

GLASS IS THE MOST VARIED IN APPEARANCE of all the materials used to make beads. Glass can be clear and brilliantly transparent, reflecting the world around it; mysteriously translucent, emanating a rich glow from within; or even as opaque as stone. It can be vibrantly colored, thanks to the addition of particular minerals (iron for green, cobalt for blue, and so on) or metallic oxides. Its surface can be shiny or matte, and within it can encase layers of color and pattern. Glass can be embellished and textured with ribbons of molten glass or it can be coated with lustrous metallic finishes. Glass can even be cut and faceted like precious stones.

This versatile material can take on many different appearances and yet it is made from a relatively simple formula: Mix a certain proportion of silica (quartz sand) with lime and soda or potash. Then fire until these ingredients fuse and become transparent. Sounds simple, yes? It seems wondrous, however, that early civilizations could have discovered the alchemy to convert humble sand into beautiful and durable glass. The ancients began creating glass beads before 2000 B.C., most likely in Sumeria or Mesopotamia. Through trade and conquest, glass beads have traveled far throughout the world and throughout time.

As ancient as glass beads are in origin, they continue to evolve and to enrich today's beaded jewelry designs. To fashion a **Classic** piece, you might mix art nouveau–inspired filigree brass with deep red fire-polished glass beads and lampworked golden flowers. Or perhaps a **Special Occasion** will inspire you to make a scene-stealing necklace of blue and green Venetian foil-lined glass beads. And for a **Fashion-Forward** mood, bright multicolored seed bead ruffles will add an "Olé" touch to a bracelet showcasing one-of-a-kind, brilliant lampworked beads.

As you explore some of the faces of glass in the jewelry designs within this book, we hope you will expand your glass vocabulary. No other man-made material will give you more ways to express your ideas for beautiful jewelry!

The Many Facets of
Glass

Before the advent of glassmaking, obsidian was nature's glass, prized for its durability and shining dark beauty. It was used in weapons, as well as for objects of personal adornment. The oldest known man-made glass beads date back to around 2200 B.C. They were the first glass objects to be made by Sumerian and Mesopotamian craftsmen. Although there were various historic centers of glassmaking over time, such as ancient Egypt, the Roman Empire, and Renaissance Venice, styles, colors, patterns, and glassmaking techniques were disbursed throughout the ancient world— including Africa—via trade. Even those world travelers, the Vikings, bought, traded for, and eventually made glass beads.

Today's glass artists use many of the same techniques developed by the ancients to produce both manufactured and studio art glass beads. Whether glass beads are used as humble accents in beaded jewelry, as a seed-bead base to be embellished, or as a focal point in a design, they add timeless beauty to any design.

Glass Beadmaking Techniques

The formula to make *primary glasswork* (glass made from raw materials) is basic and has remained virtually unchanged over millennia. Combine silica (which is a *former*) with potash (a *flux,* which allows the silica to melt at a lower temperature) plus limestone (a *stabilizer,* which makes the glass uniform) and heat until it melts. *Secondary glasswork* is the manufacture of finished glass pieces from glass stock such as rods, sheet, or *cullet* (glass pellets).

Manufactured glass objects are formed by blowing glass into molds—usually for thin-walled items such as bottles, pressing it into molds, drawing it (this produces tubes, sheet glass, and rods), or casting centrifugally. Once the melted glass has been formed, it is annealed by placing it in a hot kiln and gradually reducing the temperature to cool the glass slowly. Sometimes glass is reheated in order to shape it by bending, sagging, pressing, or blowing.

Glass, which is strong and durable when cooled, can then be etched, carved, faceted, sanded, or drilled. Any gem-cutting technique can be applied to glass. After all, silica, the mineral that forms glass, is quartz, which ranks 7 out of 10 on the Moh's Hardness Scale.

The following types of glass beads demonstrate the variety of ways that glass can be shaped and formed, whether by machine or by the hand of the artisan.

Blown-glass beads are formed by inflating a molten ball **(gather or gob)** at the end of a blowpipe. This process occurs over a handheld torch **(flameworking or lamp-working)**. The glass is then blown free-form or blown into a mold to create beads of uniform size and shape. Types of glass used are either "soft" glass or "hard" boro-silicate glass, the latter of which can withstand sudden changes of temperature.

ˇ
ˇ

ˆ
ˆ

Cast- or powdered-glass beads are produced by grinding recycled glass (usually from bottles) into a fine powder, then firing the powder in a mold. Most such beads are made in West Africa.

Drawn or furnace beads are made by pulling a gather of molten glass with a bubble in opposite directions until a thin, hollow tube is formed. The long tube is cut into canes and then further cut into beads, which are finally tumbled or ground to the desired shape and finish. The process is very much the same as it was in ancient times and allows for the production of numerous beads in a short time. Seed beads are one of the most common forms of drawn beads.

ˇ
ˇ

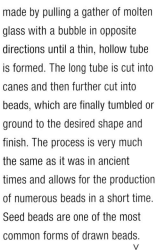

Pressed beads are machine-formed by pouring molten glass into metal molds. The Czech Republic is best known for these popular beads, which can be found in both vintage and contemporary forms and colors. The beads are often faceted and **fire-polished** (reheated to smooth the surface and add shine) and come in seem-ingly endless varieties of colors.

ˇ
ˇ

Wound glass beads require a very labor-intensive process of winding molten glass around a metallic rod (mandrel). There is no need to drill a hole in the bead with this method since winding the glass around the mandrel automatically creates one. Traditionally, the molten glass was extracted from a crucible in a furnace—a technique still practiced in India and Africa.

∨
∨

Lampworked beads by Michael Barley.

∧
∧

Lampworked beads are created by melting glass rods over a torch and winding them around a mandrel. This furnace-free method of making wound beads revolutionized beadmaking in Venice in the sixteenth century because beads could be produced in small cottage industries rather than large, organized environments. Early lampworkers heated their glass rods over oil lamps—thus, the term "lampworked." Today's lampwork artists produce beautiful beads with signature looks, from encased images to surface embellishments.

Mosaic beads (also called millefiori for "thousand flowers"), which are both drawn and wound, were invented during the first millennium B.C. in western Asia. The colorful, richly patterned beads are created by fusing multi-hued glass canes, often over a base of plain wound glass. Canes are first layered to produce a cross-sectioned pattern. Then, the glass bundle is heated, at which time it is stretched to produce a fused cane. Everything from geometric patterns to faces can be created with this technique.

It's remarkable, really, how glass beads encapsulate something as vast as thousands of years of history and artistry. The variety of ways in which artisans can approach technique and design when making glass beads is ever-evolving. And yet, even with modern refinements in glass-making techniques and design, many of today's beads resemble their ancient counterparts. When we make jewelry with glass beads, we celebrate timeless beauty.

∨
∨

Murano, Island of Glass

In Renaissance Europe, Venice emerged as the capitol of glassmaking. It is likely that the earlier Roman period of glassmaking paved the way for Venice to rise to primacy, as did the Mongol conquest of the Islamic world in 1401, which ended that civilization's glass industry. Although glass production had occurred in Venice from circa A.D. 600, it reached new heights at this time. In 1292, all the Venetian glass factories were moved to the island of Murano, which was a short boat ride from the city. The move served two purposes: It isolated the risk of fire from the ever-burning furnaces, and it kept glassmaking techniques secret. Secrecy was so important, in fact, that glassworkers faced death if they revealed trade secrets or left the island to set up competitive operations.

Until Venice's defeat by Napoleon in 1797, the quantity and beauty of glass traded by the seafaring Venetians was unmatched. One of their most important technical innovations was the advent of drawn glass. Wound glass was a labor-intensive process in which a single worker wound molten glass around a metal rod or wire (no hole had to be drilled in a bead since the rod created one). Drawn glass was a cheaper, faster process. Hollow glass globes were stretched into long hollow tubes—two men, each holding a metal plate attached to the molten glass, ran in opposite directions. The tubes were stretched to a length of about 300 feet and were then cut into canes, which were eventually made into beads. Experts estimate that more than 100,000 varieties of bead types and designs were produced in Murano and Venice during this period.

When glassmaking in Venice was again permitted in the late sixteenth century, lamp-wound or lampworked beads became an important cottage industry. They did not require the large furnaces and workforce of drawn beads and were made simply by winding molten glass above oil lamps.

Ten chevron beads from seventeenth-century Venice.
Collection of The Corning Museum of Glass, Corning, NY.

the
projects

classic

As you finish wrapping the vintage blue vase, you imagine how beautiful this will look filled with a fresh spray of flowers from your friends' new garden. For the past two years, they have searched for the perfect starter home. Today you will join others for a joyous housewarming party for the excited couple. Before you head out, you'll also grab the traditional loaf of bread and bag of salt—guaranteeing a future of good luck and happiness!

Whenever you share one of life's important events with friends or family, you let them know how much you care by your gifts, your presence, and by the way in which you adorn yourself. After all, wearing something beyond the everyday sends a loving message: You honor them. Even if the festivities are casual, why not add a multistrand, opulent necklace of turquoise and muscovite to your simple white shirt and slacks?

Many such **Classic** occasions are, however, not casual at all. And it's very likely that there will be lots of photos taken to commemorate a housewarming or similar gathering. If you are sporting lovely hammered-silver earring hoops that are dripping with tourmaline and garnet dangles, you'll shine. A romantic lariat of peach moonstone and jasper is also a choice that will wear well over time and for many future celebrations.

Africa Calls

The energy of this bright piece brings to mind a busy international marketplace. Italian lampworked beads and a handmade silver clasp from Thailand enhance the main attraction—trade beads from Africa—in this sunny bracelet.

MATERIALS

About 40 size 11° yellow with green stripe African trade beads (A)

About 120 size 10° white with blue and red stripe African trade beads (B)

About 260 size 8° yellow with red and green stripe African trade beads (C)

About 110 size 8° white with blue stripe African trade beads (D)

About 35 size 6° yellow with red, white, and blue stripe African trade beads (E)

3 red 8mm millefiori rounds

3 white 8mm millefiori rounds

1 Thai silver 2" (5cm) 7-strand hook-and-eye clasp

Yellow size D, 6lb test FireLine braided beading thread

TOOLS

Scissors

Size 10 beading needle

FINISHED SIZE

6½" (17cm)

Note: African trade beads are not always uniform in size, so it may be necessary to adjust numbers while stringing beads in Step 6 and on.

1 Use the needle and a comfortable long length of thread to string a tension bead, leaving a 12" (31cm) tail. Use flat peyote stitch to form a strip 19 beads long by 6 rows deep:

Rows 1 and 2: String 20C.

Row 3: Pass back through the eighteenth bead strung. String 1C and pass back through the sixteenth bead strung. Repeat, stringing 1C and passing back through every other bead strung for the entire row. Weave thread through the first three beads strung and pass through the bead resting under the third bead strung. Pass back through the second and first beads strung and pass back through the final bead strung (Figure 1).

Figure 1

Row 4: String 1C and pass back through the next bead in Row 3. Repeat for the length of the row.

Row 5: Repeat Row 3.

Row 6: Repeat Row 4.

2 Use the working thread to weave through beads so that the thread is exiting the middle bead on the end of the strip. String 1C, 1 white millefiori round, 1C, and 1B. Pass back through the C, round, and C. Weave thread through the strip and stitch through all of the beads just strung again to reinforce. Weave in thread, tying half-hitch knots to secure and trim thread. Repeat on the other side of the strip, using the tail end of the thread and a red millefiori round.

3 Repeat Steps 1 and 2 to form a second strip 19 beads long by 6 rows deep.

4 Repeat Steps 1 and 2, stringing 22C for Rows 1 and 2 to form a strip 21 beads long by 6 rows deep.

5 Use a comfortable length of thread to string the center bead on one side of the 21-bead strip. Tie a surgeon's knot to secure. String 6E and pass through the center bead on one side of the 19-bead strip. Pass back through the 6E and pass through the bead on the 21-bead strip again (Figure 2). Pass through all of the beads used in this step again to reinforce.

6 Weave through two beads in the 21-bead strip. String 7D and pass through the 19-bead strip, two beads from the bead used in Step 5. Pass through all of the beads in this step again to reinforce.

7 Repeat Step 6 using 9C.

8 Repeat Step 6 using 10B.

9 Repeat Step 6 using 10A.

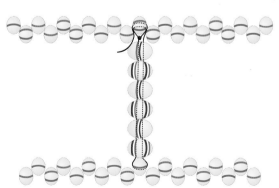

Figure 2

10 Repeat Steps 6–9 on the other side of the strand formed in Step 5.

11 Repeat Steps 5–10 to connect the other 19-bead strip to the other side of the 21-bead strip.

12 Use a long, comfortable length of thread to string 5E and the middle loop of one half of the clasp, leaving a 6" (15cm) tail thread. Pass back through the 5E. String 6E and pass through the center bead on one side of one 19-bead-long strip. Pass back through the 6E and use the working and tail ends of the thread to tie a surgeon's knot (Figure 3).

13 Pass back through the 6E and weave through beads in the strip to exit three beads from the strand formed in Step 5. String 14D and pass through the next loop of the clasp. Pass through all of the beads and the loop again to reinforce.

14 Repeat Step 13 using 14C and the next loop of the clasp.

15 Repeat Step 13 using 18B and the end loop of the clasp.

16 Repeat Steps 13–15 on the other side of the strand formed in Step 12.

17 Repeat Steps 12–16 to attach the other half of the clasp to the other 19-bead strip.

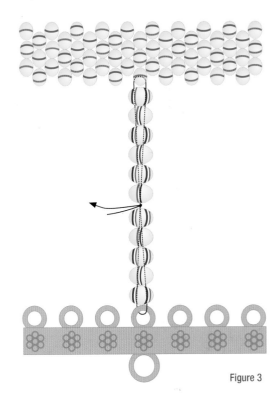

Figure 3

Honey Blossoms

Three designs of lampworked glass beads by Patti Cahill in sugary shades of pink and yellow are enticing for brass bee charms. Attached to a tassel of mixed brass chains, the bees fly up toward their nectar in these eye-catching earrings.

MATERIALS

12 dandelion rainbow frost size 11° seed beads

2 coral with yellow and fuchsia dotted 6.5x10mm lampworked glass rondelles

2 coral with yellow and fuchsia leafed 7x12mm lampworked glass rondelles

2 coral with yellow and fuchsia swirled 7x12mm lampworked glass rondelles

2 natural brass 18x14mm bee charms

4" (10cm) of natural brass unsoldered delicate curb chain

4" (10cm) of natural brass unsoldered rollo chain

4" (10cm) of natural brass unsoldered ornate chain

1 pair natural brass long arched ear wires

12" (31cm) of gunmetal 22-gauge wire

TOOLS

Wire cutters

Chain-nose pliers

Flat-nose pliers

Round-nose pliers

FINISHED SIZE

5" (13cm)

1 Cut the chains in half.

2 Use 3" (8cm) of wire to form a 6mm wrapped loop that attaches to one end of one piece of each type of chain. String 1 seed bead, 1 swirled glass rondelle, and 1 seed bead. Form a wrapped loop.

3 Use 3" (8cm) of wire to form a wrapped loop that attaches to the previous wrapped loop. String 1 seed bead, 1 leafed glass rondelle, and 1 seed bead. Form a wrapped loop that attaches to 1 ear wire.

4 Open the ear wire and use the pointed end to string 1 seed bead, 1 dotted rondelle, and 1 seed bead.

5 Open the middle link of ornate chain. String 1 bee charm and close the chain.

6 Repeat Steps 1–5 to form a second earring.

My Nest

Seed beads and Czech pressed glass in soothing hues of blue and green create the perfect environment for pewter birds and their nest. The back of the nest reads "home" and, when blended with the unique herringbone-stitched pieces in the necklace, reinforces the notion that home is where the heart is.

MATERIALS

About 5 g matte aqua gray size 15° seed beads (A)

About 5 g jade gray size 15° seed beads (B)

About 5 g sage size 15° seed beads (C)

About 10 g dark green opaque luster size 11° seed beads (D)

25 pale green 4x6mm fire-polished rondelles

20 seafoam green 3x8mm discs

9 swirled white and teal 12mm Czech pressed-glass squares

1 pewter 15mm nest with eggs bead

1 pewter 25x8mm sparrow bird bead

2 pewter 8x22mm flying bird beads

1 sterling silver 25mm bird toggle clasp

2 sterling silver 2mm crimp tubes

2 sterling silver 4mm crimp covers

21" (53cm) of silver .019 beading wire

Pale green size D Nymo beading thread

TOOLS

Scissors

Size 13 beading needle

Size 11 beading needle

Wire cutters

Crimping pliers

FINISHED SIZE

17¾" (45cm)

1 **Row 1:** Centerpiece tube: Use single-needle ladder stitch to form a chain of 8C, leaving a 12" (31cm) tail thread. Connect the chain to form a ring, making sure not to twist the beads, with the needle exiting one bead.

2 **Row 2:** String 2C and pass down through the next bead in the ring. Pass up through the next bead in the ring, string 2C, and pass down through the next bead in the ring (Figure 1). Repeat around the ring.

Figure 1

Rows 3–6: Repeat Row 2, using all C beads.

Rows 7 and 8: Repeat Row 2, alternating C and B beads.

Rows 9–14: Repeat Row 2, using all B beads.

Rows 15 and 16: Repeat Row 2, alternating B and A beads.

Rows 17–22: Repeat Row 2, using all A beads.

Rows 23 and 24: Repeat Row 2, alternating A and D beads.

Rows 25–27: Repeat Row 2, using all D beads.

Row 28: Repeat Row 2, alternating A and D beads.

Rows 29–34: Repeat Row 2, blending A, B, and C beads.

Rows 35–40: Repeat Row 2, using all D beads.

Rows 41–74: Repeat Rows 2–34, reversing the sequence.

Row 75: Repeat Row 2.

3 Picot: String 5A and pass down through the next C in Row 75. Pass up through the next C. Repeat around the tube to add four fringe ends.

4 Center Embellishment: Weave thread through the tube to exit the top of one bead in Row 40. String 1A, 1B, and 1C and pass through the same bead again. Pass through the bead above it, in Row 39. String 1A, 1B, and 1C. Pass through the bead in Row 39 again and pass through the bead above it, in Row 38. Repeat three times, for rows 37, 36, and 35, making sure to stay on the same column of beads. Skip 1 column and repeat entire step. Skip 1 column and repeat again. Weave in thread end, tying half-hitch knots between several beads to secure, and trim (Figure 2).

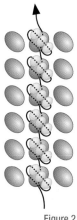

Figure 2

5 Use the tail thread to repeat Step 3 on the other end of the tube. Weave in thread end, tying half-hitch knots between several beads to secure, and trim.

6 Tassels: To form the tassel that hangs from Rows 29–34 of the tube, string 13D. Wrap the D around the tube and pass through all of the D again to form a ring around the tube. Tie a surgeon's knot.

7 String 1D, 1 glass rondelle, 1 glass disc, 1 glass square, 1 glass disc, 1 glass rondelle, 1D, 1 flying bird, 1D, and 16B. Skip 3B (to form a picot) and pass back through all of the beads in this step.

8 String 14D and wrap the beads around the tube on the right side of the ring formed in Step 6. Pass through all of the beads in the tassel from the first D to the last D. String 16A. Skip 3A and pass back through all of the beads.

9 Repeat Step 8, wrapping the 14D on the other side of the ring formed in Step 6 and using C beads for the picot fringe.

10 Pass through the 13 beads in the ring formed in Step 6 and all of the beads in the tassel. String 16B. Skip 3B and pass back through all beads to the tail thread. Use the working and tail threads to tie a surgeon's knot. Use a thread burner to trim threads.

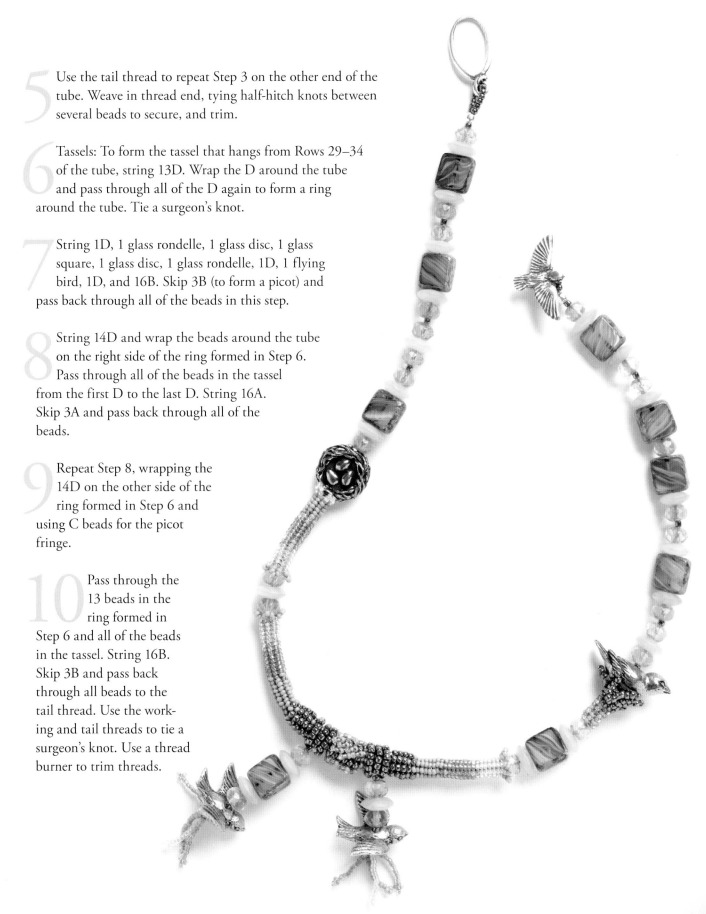

11 Repeat Steps 6–10 on the other side of the center section of the tube and omitting the glass square and 1 glass disc from the tassel.

12 Short tube: Repeat Steps 1 and 2 using A beads.

Rows 3–5: Repeat Row 2 using A beads.

Rows 6–8: Repeat Row 2 using A, B, and C beads.

Rows 9–13: Repeat Row 2 using B beads.

Rows 14–16: Repeat Row 2 using A, B, and C beads.

Rows 17–21: Repeat Row 2, using C beads.

13 Use the working thread to repeat Step 3, adding a picot of A beads. Use the tail thread to repeat Step 3, adding a picot of C beads.

14 **Perch:** Repeat Steps 1 and 2 using A, B, and C beads.

Rows 3–6: Repeat Row 2 using A, B, and C beads.

Row 7: Repeat Row 2, using A, B, and C beads with a D bead between each size 15° seed bead.

Rows 8 and 9: Repeat Row 2 using D beads.

Row 10: Repeat Row 2, using D beads, and string three beads every time instead of two to form an increase.

Row 11: Repeat Row 2 using D beads.

15 **Picot:** Repeat Step 3, using D beads, and adding 8 picot ends around the tube.

16 Use the beading wire to string 1 crimp tube, 12 size 11° seed beads, and the ring half of the clasp. Pass back through the tube and crimp. Cover the tube with a crimp cover.

17 String 1 size 11° seed bead, 1 glass rondelle, 1 glass disc, 1 glass square, 1 glass disc, and 1 glass rondelle twice. String 1 size 11° seed bead , 1 glass rondelle, 1 glass disc, 1 glass rondelle, 1 size 11° seed bead, 1 glass rondelle, 1 glass disc, 1 glass square, 1 glass disc, 1 glass rondelle, the pewter nest, and the short tube. String enough size 11° seed beads to fill the tube (about 20). String 1 glass rondelle, 1 glass disc, 1 glass rondelle, and the centerpiece tube. String enough size 11° seed beads to fill the focal piece (about 75). String 1 glass rondelle, 1 glass disc, 1 glass square, 1 glass disc, 1 glass rondelle, and the perch. String enough size 11° seed beads to fill the perch (about 10). String the pewter sparrow, 1 size 11° seed bead, 1 glass rondelle, 1 glass disc, 1 glass rondelle, 1 size 11° seed bead, 1 glass rondelle, 1 glass disc, 1 glass square, 1 glass disc, 1 glass rondelle, 1 size 11° seed bead, 1 glass rondelle, 1 glass square, 1 glass rondelle, 1 glass square, 1 glass disc, 1 glass rondelle, 1 size 11° seed bead, 1 glass rondelle, 1 glass disc, 1 glass square, 1 glass disc, 1 glass rondelle, 1 size 11° seed bead, 1 crimp tube, 12 size 11° seed beads and the bird half of the clasp. Pass back through the tube; crimp and cover.

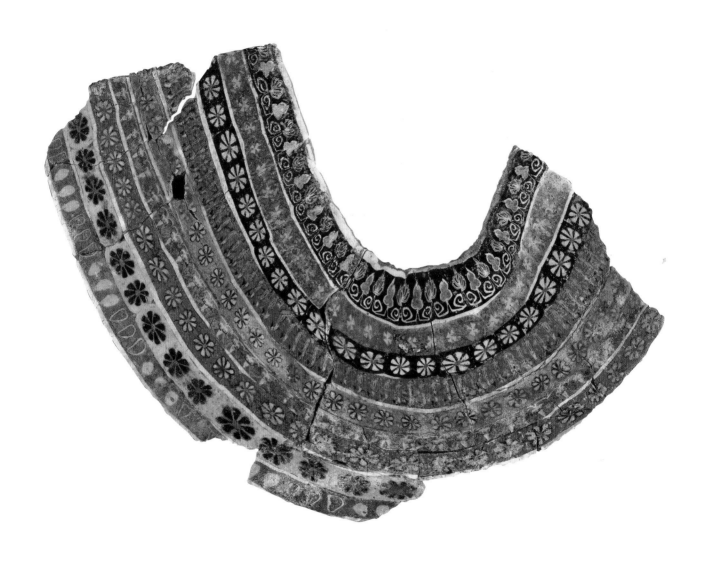

This inlay in the form of a collar dates to sometime between the third to first century B.C. in Alexandria. It features multicolored fused and preformed canes, with floral patterns. Collection of The Corning Museum of Glass, Corning, NY.

did you know . . .

Egypt and the First Great Age of Glass

During the New Kingdom period in ancient Egypt (circa 1350 B.C.), the world's first glassmaking epoch emerged. In this period, Egypt enjoyed great wealth and security—the perfect conditions in which to develop a sophisticated and rich material culture. Royal and noble Egyptians used beads to cover most articles of clothing as well as to adorn their bodies, including in death. In fact, royal patronage allowed Egyptian glassmakers to advance their arts to a high level. At first, glass was an exotic, coveted material, made exclusively for the pharaohs and their courts. As the making of glass proliferated, wealthier commoners were able to acquire glass as well. Egyptians loved their deeply colored stones—especially carnelian, turquoise, and lapis lazuli. Soon, glassmakers began producing opaque glass that imitated these favorites and, in many cases, replaced them. After the end of the Nineteenth Dynasty (circa 1200 B.C.), the glass industry declined. It would not revive until the fourth century B.C., when Alexander the Great conquered Egypt and founded Alexandria, an international center of trade.

MATERIALS

About 45 electric blue magic lined
   size 8° seed beads

11 blue 7mm Czech pressed-glass
   rounds

8 assorted brown, cream, black,
   and blue 10–12mm African
   trade beads

1 black striped 16x20mm African
   trade bead bicone

6 yellow 14x16mm Javanese lampworked glass melon beads

2 cream with blue dots 15x18mm
   Venetian lampworked glass
   beads

4 sunset 14mm polymer clay
   rounds

2 cobalt 14mm polymer clay
   rounds

1 natural brass 33x43mm Asian
   marine dolphin pendant

13 natural brass 4mm melon beads

22 natural brass 7mm hobnail bead
   caps

10 natural brass 15mm promise
   connectors

12 natural brass 9mm etched jump
   rings

1 natural brass 24x11mm hook
   clasp

4 natural brass crimp covers

2 copper 2x3mm crimp tubes

24" (61cm) of antique brass .024
   beading wire

TOOLS

Wire cutters

Chain-nose pliers

Flat-nose pliers (or two pairs of
   chain-nose pliers)

Crimping pliers

FINISHED SIZE

22" (56cm)

Ocean Journey

Glass beads made in the Czech Republic, Africa, Indonesia, and Italy blend with polymer clay beads handmade by artist Pam Wynn, giving this piece a truly global view. The brass dolphin pendant works wonders as a clasp that can float around the neck in order to showcase any and all of the lovely beads.

1 Open 1 jump ring and attach it to a second jump ring. Open a third jump ring, pass it through the first and second jump rings, and close the ring to form a three-ring flower (Figure 1). Repeat entire step for a total of 4 flowers.

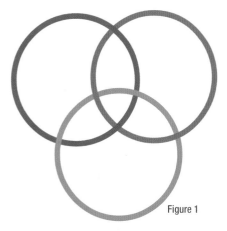

Figure 1

2 Use the wire to string 1 crimp tube and the hook clasp. Pass back through the tube and crimp. String 2 crimp covers.

3 String 1 bead cap, 1 pressed-glass round, 1 bead cap, 1 brass melon round, 1 African trade bead, 1 brass melon round, 1 African trade bead, 1 brass melon round, 1 bead cap, 1 pressed-glass round, 1 bead cap, and 1 Javanese glass melon bead three times, omitting the final Javanese glass melon bead.

4 String 1 sunset polymer round, 1 promise connector, 1 Venetian glass bead, 1 promise connector, and 1 sunset polymer round.

5 String 1 bead cap, 1 pressed-glass round, 1 bead cap, 1 Javanese glass melon bead, 1 promise connector, 1 cobalt polymer round, 1 promise connector, 1 Javanese glass melon bead, 1 bead cap, 1 pressed-glass round, and 1 bead cap.

6 String 1 brass melon round, 1 African trade bead, 1 brass melon round, 1 of the jump-ring flowers formed in Step 1, 1 promise connector, 1 jump-ring flower, the black striped 16×20mm African trade bead bicone, 1 jump-ring flower, 1 promise connector, 1 jump-ring flower, 1 brass melon round, 1 African trade bead, and 1 brass melon round.

7 Repeat Step 5. Repeat Step 4.

8 String 1 bead cap, 1 pressed-glass round, 1 bead cap, 2 crimp covers and 1 crimp tube. Pass the wire around the body of the Asian marine dolphin pendant. Pass back through the tube and crimp. Slide the crimp covers over the crimp tube.

did you know . . .

Ancient Romans—Masters of Glass

The second great age of glass belongs to the Romans (100 B.C. to A.D. 400). They were the ancient world's greatest producers and users of glass—in the first century A.D., more glass was made than in the previous fifteen centuries. Glass was used for everything from jewelry to bowls and vessels to burial urns. Instead of the traditional ceramic tesserae (small tiles), Roman craftsmen began to use glass tesserae in their elaborate architectural mosaics. They were also the greatest glass innovators, appropriating and developing most of the decorative techniques used by today's glassmakers. This was due in part to the enormous geographical range of their empire, which included Syria, Egypt, Switzerland, Italy, the Rhineland, France, and England. They imposed their cultural identity throughout the ancient world. They also absorbed other cultures and technologies through domination and trade.

The Roman glass industry, like so many other enterprises that civilization engaged in, was vast and efficient. The most significant technological leap came in around 50 B.C. by way of the Syro-Palestine glasshouses. Free-blowing transformed glassmaking, speeding the process itself and allowing for more fluid shapes and thinner glass walls in finished pieces. Before that time, glass items were either wound around a clay core (which was then scraped out of the fired item) or cast into molds.

Throughout the ancient world, Roman beads were prized for their diverse colors and patterns, as well as for the complex techniques used to make them. Mosaic face cane beads and checkerboard cane beads were particular favorites.

Detail from the cup above.

Passionflower

A blend of lampworked glass, pressed glass, and brass flowers make up this stunning necklace. Brass filigree wrapped around glass rings create vintage-looking focal points whose classic charm perfectly balances the look of the bright lampworked glass flowers.

MATERIALS

24 orange 3x7mm Czech pressed-glass flower beads

19 orange/clear/green 6x8mm Czech pressed-glass rondelles

5 orange/clear 25mm lampworked flower beads

2 orange 20mm glass rings

1 orange 35mm glass ring

34 dark copper bronze-plated size 11° metal seed beads

38 natural brass 6mm daisy bead caps

24 natural brass 6mm blossom bead caps

2 natural brass 35mm violet petal filigree

2 natural brass 45mm passionflower filigree

1 natural brass 10x24mm swirl hook-and-eye clasp

2 natural brass 15mm jump rings

12 natural brass 1x2mm crimp beads

1 natural brass 2" (5cm) head pin

27" (69cm) of antique brass .019 beading wire

TOOLS

Wire cutters

Crimping pliers

Chain-nose pliers

Round-nose pliers

Nylon-jaw pliers

FINISHED SIZE

18" (46cm)

1. Place 1 passionflower filigree on top of the 35mm glass ring. Use your fingers to curve the top two and bottom two petals around the glass ring. Carefully turn the filigree and ring over and place the other passionflower filigree on top of the ring so that the petals of the second filigree sit between the petals of the first filigree. Use your fingers to wrap the middle-right and middle-left petals around the ring.

2. Use one 15mm jump ring to connect the filigree to the glass ring by passing through the right side of the front top center filigree petal just below the glass ring and the right side of the back filigree petal to the left of the front top center petal. Repeat to attach the second 15mm jump ring on the left side of the front top center filigree petal (Figure 1).

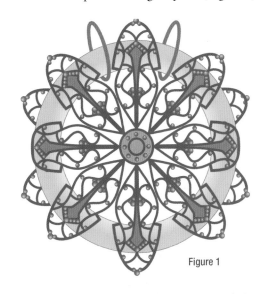

Figure 1

3 Place 1 violet petal filigree face down on your work surface. Place one 20mm glass ring on the filigree. Hold the two pieces with your non-dominant hand and use your dominant hand to carefully curve the petals of the filigree around the ring. If necessary, use nylon-jaw pliers to secure the filigree more tightly to the ring. Repeat for the second ring and filigree.

4 Use 9" (23cm) of wire to string 1 crimp tube, 1 seed bead, 1 crimp tube, and 1 violet petal filigree/20mm glass ring, wrapping the wire around the ring so that it hides between two of the filigree petals (Figure 2). Pass back through the crimp tube, seed bead, and crimp tube. Use chain-nose pliers to flatten the crimp tubes. String 1 seed bead.

5 String 1 daisy bead cap, 1 Czech flower, 1 blossom bead cap, 1 rondelle, 1 blossom bead cap, 1 Czech flower, and 1 daisy bead cap.

6 String 1 seed bead, 1 lampworked flower, and 1 seed bead. Repeat Step 5.

7 String 2 seed beads, 1 jump ring on the pendant, 1 daisy bead cap, 1 rondelle, 1 daisy bead cap, the other jump ring on the pendant, and 2 seed beads.

8 Repeat Step 5. Repeat Step 6. Repeat Step 4, reversing the stringing sequence and attaching the wire to the other violet petal filigree/20mm glass ring.

9 Repeat Step 4, using the opposite side of the first violet petal filigree/20mm ring. Repeat Step 5. Repeat Step 6.

Figure 2

10 String 1 seed bead, 1 daisy bead cap, 1 rondelle, 1 daisy bead cap, and 1 seed bead.

11 Repeat Steps 5 and 10 twice. String 1 crimp tube, 1 seed bead, 1 crimp tube, and one half of the clasp. Pass back through the crimp tube, seed bead, and crimp tube. Use chain-nose pliers to flatten the crimp tubes.

12 Repeat Step 9 using the second violet petal filigree/20mm jump ring. Repeat Steps 10 and 11 for the other half of the necklace.

13 Use the head pin to string 1 seed bead, 1 lampworked flower, and 1 seed bead. Form a wrapped-loop that attaches to the eye half of the clasp.

TINY GEMS

Many theorists in the past pointed to old windows as evidence that glass flows at room temperature. Although it is a molten liquid when it is initially formed, glass that has cooled and hardened is a solid. The uneven thickness of old glass, which is often wavy in texture as well, is the result of the way the glasses were made, not the movement of glass molecules at room temperatures.

Autumn Heart

MATERIALS

About 440 matte elderberry size 15°
  seed beads (A)
About 100 petunia size 15° seed
  beads (B)
About 100 lavender mist size 15°
  seed beads (C)
14 purple 6x15mm Czech pressed-
  glass bamboo tubes
1 purple 35x50mm borosilicate lampworked glass heart pendant
1 sterling silver 12x18mm paisley
  toggle clasp
4 sterling silver 2mm crimp tubes
4 sterling silver 3.4mm crimp covers
8¼" (21cm) of sterling silver 2.25mm
  double cable chain
16" (41cm) of .019 Soft Touch
  beading wire
About 60" (152cm) of crystal-clear
  6lb test FireLine braided beading
  thread

TOOLS

Wire cutters
Crimping pliers
Scissors
Size 12 beading needle

FINISHED SIZE

18" (46cm)

Albert Camus described autumn as "A second spring when every leaf's a flower." The borosilicate glass heart made by Brent Graber is a beautiful example of all the colors of the most colorful season. Tiny seed beads in subtly different shades of purple embellish a chain, creating the perfect backdrop for nature's splendor.

1 Use 8" (20cm) of wire to string 1 crimp tube and one half of the clasp. Pass back through the tube and crimp. Cover the tube with a crimp cover.

2 String 1 pressed-glass bamboo tube and 1A six times. String 1 pressed-glass bamboo tube, 1 crimp tube, and one end of the chain. Pass back through the tube and crimp. Cover the tube with a crimp cover.

3 Use the chain to string the borosilicate lampworked glass heart pendant.

4 Repeat Steps 1 and 2 using the other half of the clasp and the other end of the chain.

5 Tie one end of 30" (76cm) of the braided beading thread to one end of the chain using a surgeon's knot and leaving a 6" (15cm) tail.

6 String 7A. Pass through the fifth chain link.

7 Repeat Step 6 fourteen times, skipping four chain links between each thread pass.

8 Repeat Step 6 fifteen times back up the chain toward the crimp tube and passing the thread through the same chain links in the opposite direction.

9 Pass through the first 2A string in Step 6. String 3B and pass through the sixth and seventh A and the chain link (Figure 1).

10 Repeat Step 9 fourteen times.

Figure 1

11 Repeat Step 9 fifteen times using C beads, going back up the chain toward the crimp tube and passing the thread through the same chain links in the opposite direction.

12 Slide the heart pendant down to the center of the chain so that it rests against the seed-beaded section of chain. Weave in thread ends, tying several surgeon's knots between beads to secure.

13 Repeat Steps 5–12, beginning on the other end of the chain.

did you know . . .

Queen of Costume Jewelry—Miriam Haskell (1899–1981)

From 1926 to the late 1940s, Miriam Haskell's jewelry company produced works that elevated the beauty and status of costume jewelry in the United States. Although she herself was not a jewelry designer, Haskell hired Frank Hess as her chief designer (he stayed in this position until 1960). Hess's innovative designs and the hallmark quality of materials and construction in each piece earned Haskell's company a premier reputation—including with fashion-conscious women such as the Duchess of Windsor, as well as with movie stars.

The glass pearls that were used in much of Haskell's jewelry set the standard for beautiful, well-crafted imitations. Haskell traveled abroad regularly to find the best materials. Fine-quality glass pearls originally came from Gablonz in Bohemia (today's Czech Republic). In the late 1930s and again after World War II, Haskell sourced most of her faux seed and baroque pearls from Japan. Additionally, glass beads from Murano and faceted crystals from Austria were star performers in the company's glass-rich creations.

Vintage pieces from the company's first twenty years are extremely collectable and command high prices. Haskell retired in 1950, selling the business to her brother. Today, Miriam Haskell jewelry is still produced, although the company has been sold several times and is no longer in the Haskell family.

This Miriam Haskell necklace contains several varieties of glass beads that were common to the company's costume jewelry designs: glass seed pearls, glass baroque pearls, and glass crystals.

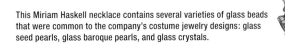

special-occasion

I t took you years to fill your garage and basement with all your found treasures. You've loved the hunt—going to garage sales, flea markets, auctions, and secondhand stores that became your favorite haunts. Friends often sought you out when they wanted to know whether a vase was a real arts-and-crafts period piece or whether a carved mahogany chair inherited from relatives had any value beyond the sentimental. Over time, you learned from dealers, books, and television series devoted to collectibles. Most of all, you learned from seeing and touching these items from the past. It never occurred to you that you might just be building a second career in the process.

Today you're opening the doors of your own small antique shop. All that "dusty junk," as some described it, has been polished, shined, and arranged to create an exciting journey through time. Champagne has been chilled and tiny madeleines are arranged on fine silver platters. Cut-crystal bowls hold mounds of grapes. After a month of cleaning, painting, and hanging old chandeliers in a quaint storefront, you're eager to launch your own business.

This definitely calls for wearing **Special-Occasion** jewelry. Dangly gold filigree earrings with bright blue glass discs could strike the high note you feel in your heart. Or perhaps a simple antiqued chain with a beautifully beaded flower pendant expresses your joy best. Then again, some foil-lined Venetian glass beads accented by golden branches might say what you're feeling most: You planted the seed of your new career long ago, and it's become a lovely reality.

Bollywood in Blue

Borosilicate glass beads are the stars in these dangling earrings. Gold vermeil filigree links, tiny gold beads, glass cubes, and seed beads enhance the handmade boro beads and give movement to the baubles. Whether worn by a movie star in a song-and-dance routine or by a busy woman running errands around town, these earrings are the perfect accessory.

MATERIALS

4 blue-lined crystal-clear 1.5mm glass cubes

4 purple-lined crystal-clear 1.5mm glass cubes

20 purple size 8° seed beads

4 teal and purple 18x10mm lamp-worked glass beads

16 gold-filled 2mm rounds

8 gold-filled 4mm rounds

4 gold vermeil 8x18mm oval filigree links

1 pair gold-filled French hoop ear wires with 2mm round bead

2 gold-filled 9mm jump rings

8 gold-filled 24-gauge 2" (5cm) head pins

4 gold-filled 24-gauge 2" (5cm) eye pins

12" (31cm) of gold-filled 22-gauge wire

TOOLS

Wire cutters

Chain-nose pliers

Flat-nose pliers

Round-nose pliers

FINISHED SIZE

4½" (11cm)

1 Use 1 head pin to string one 2mm gold round. Form a wrapped loop. Repeat entire step three times for a total of 4 gold dangles.

2 Use chain-nose pliers to attach the eye of the eye pin to 2 gold dangles. Use the eye pin to string 1 purple-lined crystal-clear glass cube, one 2mm gold round, 1 size 8° seed bead, one 2mm gold round, and 1 blue-lined crystal-clear glass cube. Form a wrapped loop that attaches to 1 oval filigree link.

3 Repeat Step 2, switching the placement of the purple and blue glass cubes and attaching the eye pin to a second oval filigree link.

4 Use 3" (8cm) of wire to form a wrapped loop that attaches to the tops of the oval filigree links used in Steps 2 and 3. String one 4mm gold round, 1 lampworked glass bead, and one 4mm gold round. Form a wrapped loop.

5 Use 3" (8cm) of wire to form a wrapped loop that attaches to 1 ear wire. String one 4mm gold round, 1 lampworked glass bead, and one 4mm gold round. Form a wrapped loop.

6 Use 1 jump ring to string 4 size 8° seed beads, the wrapped loop formed in Step 4, 4 size 8° seed beads, and the wrapped loop formed in Step 5.

7 Repeat Steps 1–6 to form a second earring.

TINY GEMS

In core-formed glass vessels from pre-Roman times, researchers speculate that cores were formed from animal dung.

did you know . . .

Africa and the Language of Beads

From earliest times, African people wore beads as a central expression of individual, cultural, and spiritual identity. Early beads were organic, made from such things as bone, teeth, seeds, and shells, to be followed by metal and stone beads. Later in the seventh century, glass beads arrived by way of Muslim traders. Glass beads were also traded south from Egypt (although glassmaking technology did not accompany them), as well as from India.

European explorers and traders who sailed along the west coast of Africa in the fifteenth century were quick to apprehend the riches to be taken from this continent. Gold, ivory, spices, and slaves comprised Africa's most coveted wealth. Volumes of glass beads were among the most powerful of the Europeans' bargaining chips. Beautifully patterned glass beads from Venice, including millefiori and chevron beads, together with bright multicolored seed beads, were appealing to the Africans, who loved color. Glass beads became an integral part of their extensive language of beaded clothing, objects, and jewelry. These proclaimed the wearer's economic, social, marital, and political status. Between the 1500s and 1867, slavers shipped as many as 15 million Africans to the Americas, one tragic gauge of the purchasing power of glass beads.

From the sixteenth century until today, centers of glass beadmaking in sub-Saharan Africa have been Niger, Nigeria, and Ghana. Early African glass was likely made from ground bottles, imported glass beads, or glass ingots. While the traditional methods of wound and drawn glass were used, a method of using powdered glass was developed that is virtually unique to Africa.

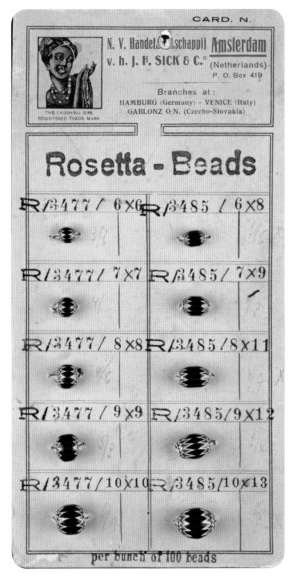

Glass chevron beads were a favorite European trade bead for Africans. Trade card of J. F. Sick & Company, The Netherlands, Amsterdam, circa 1936. Collection of The Corning Museum of Glass, Corning, NY.

Starflowers

MATERIALS

104 Cheyenne pink size 11° seed
  beads

64 cardinal size 11° seed beads

32 lilac pink mauve size 11° seed
  beads

32 golden plum size 11° seed beads

8 evening rose opal gilt-lined size 8°
  seed beads

4 mauve 4mm fire-polished glass
  rounds

4 burgundy 4mm fire-polished glass
  rounds

4 mauve/burgundy 6x8mm Czech
  pressed-glass rondelles

40 dark pink/clear 6x14mm Czech
  pressed-glass daggers

1 sterling silver 4mm jump ring

8 sterling silver 6mm jump rings

1 sterling silver 8mm jump ring

1 sterling silver 7x12mm oval lobster
  clasp

20" (51cm) of sterling silver 24-gauge
  dead-soft wire

Clear size D, 6lb test FireLine braided
  beading thread

TOOLS

Scissors

Size 12 beading needle

Wire cutters

Chain-nose pliers

Flat-nose pliers

Round-nose pliers

Thread burner

FINISHED SIZE

7¼" (18cm)

Seed beads in shades of red, pink, and plum create the 3-D centers of these funky flowers. Part delicate primrose and part outer space, the flowers make up quickly and look lovely in an all-new type of wrist corsage.

1 Use 60" (152cm) of FireLine and the beading needle to string 1 Cheyenne pink size 11° seed bead and 1 dagger ten times, leaving a 6" tail thread. Pass through all of the beads again to form a circle. Form an overhand knot to secure. Pass through one size 11° and dagger number 1 (Figure 1).

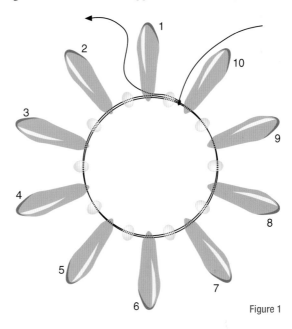

Figure 1

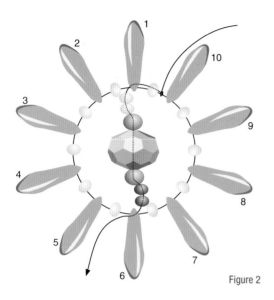

Figure 2

2 String 2 Cheyenne pink size 11° seed beads, 1 size 8° seed bead, 1 Czech pressed-glass rondelle, 1 size 8° seed bead, and 2 cardinal size 11° seed beads. Pass back through dagger number 6 (Figure 2). String 2 cardinal size 11° seed beads. Pass back through the size 8°, rondelle, and size 8°. String 2 Cheyenne pink size 11° seed beads and pass through dagger number 1, 1 seed bead, and dagger number 2 (Figure 3).

3 String 4 golden plum size 11° seed beads. Pass through the size 8°, rondelle, and size 8°. String 4 lilac pink mauve size 11° seed beads and pass back through dagger number 7. Pass back through 1 seed bead, dagger number 6, 1 seed bead, and dagger number 5. String 4 lilac pink mauve size 11° seed beads. Pass back through the size 8°, rondelle, and size 8°. String 4 golden plum size 11° seed beads and pass back through the seed bead between daggers 10 and 9 and dagger number 9 (Figure 4).

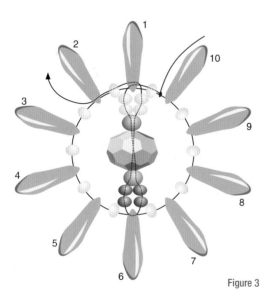

Figure 3

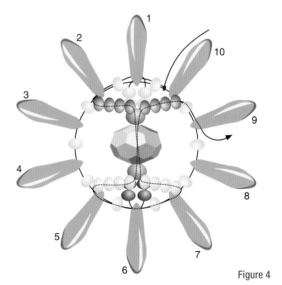

Figure 4

4 String 6 Cheyenne pink size 11° seed beads. Pass through the rondelle. String 6 cardinal size 11° seed beads and pass through dagger number 4 (Figure 5). Pass through the seed bead, dagger number 5, the seed bead, dagger number 6, the seed bead, dagger number 7, the seed bead, and dagger number 8. String 6 cardinal size 11° seed beads. Pass back through the rondelle. String 6 Cheyenne pink size 11° seed beads and pass back through dagger number 3 (Figure 6). Weave thread back to tail thread. Use both thread ends to tie a surgeon's knot. Trim using thread burner.

5 Repeat Steps 1–4 three times to make a total of 4 flowers.

6 Use 2½" (6cm) of sterling silver wire to form a wrapped loop. String 1 mauve fire-polished round and form a wrapped loop. Repeat entire step three times for a total of 4 mauve links. Set 1 link aside.

7 Use 2½" (6cm) of sterling silver to form a wrapped loop that attaches to 1 wrapped loop of 1 mauve link. String 1 burgundy fire-polished round and form a wrapped loop. Repeat entire step twice for a total of 3 chains.

8 Use 2½" (6cm) of sterling silver wire to form a wrapped loop. String 1 burgundy fire-polished round and form a wrapped loop.

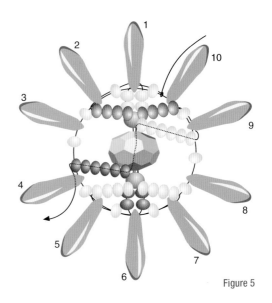

Figure 5

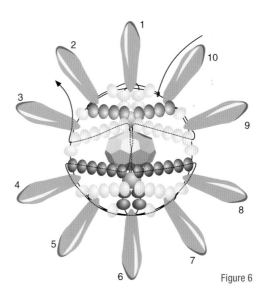

Figure 6

9 Use the 4mm jump ring to attach the lobster clasp to the burgundy link formed in Step 6. Use one 6mm jump ring to attach the other end of the burgundy link to one side of one flower.

10 Use one 6mm jump ring to attach the mauve end of one of the chains to the other side of the flower. Use one 6mm jump ring to attach the burgundy end of the chain to one side of one flower.

11 Repeat Step 10 twice.

12 Use one 6mm jump ring to attach the other side of the last flower used to the mauve link formed in Step 6. Attach the 8mm jump ring to the other end of the mauve link.

did you know . . .

Islamic Glass Beads

The last important phase in the refinement of glassmaking occurred from about 700 B.C. to A.D. 1400. At the beginning of this period, Arab armies conquered Egypt, Iran, and the Near East. Here they encountered thriving glass industries. The Islamic conquerors continued to produce large quantities of glass items, eventually introducing distinctive new forms and intricate decorations based on the four fundamental elements of Islamic art: floral, figural (stylized animal and human forms), geometric, and calligraphic. Glass from this period was patterned with feathering, festoons, and folding. Islamic glass-makers also inherited long-established traditions of cold working, which included cutting, grinding, and polishing—primary lapidary techniques. As well, they enameled and gilded the surfaces of finished glass pieces.

For Muslims, mathematics is an essential part of art and the underlying source of order in the natural world. In medieval Islamic thought, circles and spheres were the most important forms, which suggests why beads played such an important role. Beads signified status, offered protection to the wearer, and served as portable wealth.

Muslims were great mariners, who sailed the ancient world and traded extensively. Beads and other glass pieces from this era were exported as far away as China and Africa. After the Mongol conquests of western Asian in the fifteenth century, major glass production in the region ceased. Later, the luxurious and technically sophisticated glasswork of Islamic artisans from that period would be treasured by Europeans in the Middle Ages, who believed the pieces to be relics from the Holy Land.

A mosaic glass technique was used to create these ninth- to tenth-century Islamic beads from Egypt. Collection of The Corning Museum of Glass, Corning, NY. Gift of Fustat Expedition, ARCE.

Radiant Bloom

Size 11° seed beads, size 11° triangle beads, and magatamas stitched to a base of circular square stitch form the petals for this sparkly flower pendant. One flower can be stitched in less than an hour, so make one to wear on a chain as shown, make two flowers to wear as earrings, or make an entire luminous garden!

MATERIALS

About 210 clear pumpkin-lined size 11° seed beads

About 100 dark orange size 11° triangle beads

12 clear peach-lined 4mm magatamas

1 natural brass 15mm nouveau toggle ring

1 natural brass 5x30mm leaf toggle bar

2 natural brass 4mm jump rings

1 link of natural brass 7mm etched cable chain

16" (41cm) of natural brass 4x6mm flat oval chain

TOOLS

Measuring tape

Scissors

Size 13 beading needle

Chain-nose pliers

Flat-nose pliers (or second pair of chain-nose pliers)

FINISHED SIZE

16¾" (43cm)

Note: Try using other shapes of beads for the second layer of petals. Glass 1.5mm cubes work well if you use 10 beads per petal.

1 Use circular square stitch to make the base of the flower:

Round 1: String 12 size 11° seed beads. Pass through the beads again to form a circle. Tie an overhand knot. Pass through 1 bead (Figure 1).

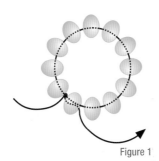

Figure 1

Figure 2

Round 2: String 2 size 11° seed beads and pass through 2 beads of the previous round (Figure 2). Repeat entire step eleven times, adding a total of 24 beads in this round. Pass through all of the beads in this round. Pass through the first bead of the round again.

Round 3: String 1 size 11° seed bead and pass through 2 beads of the previous round. Repeat. String 2 size 11° seed beads and pass through 2 beads of the previous round. Repeat entire step, adding 1 or 2 beads at a time, making sure to keep the curve of the beads flat, for a total of 28 beads in this round. Pass through all of the beads in this round. Pass through the first bead of the round again.

2 String 12 size 11° seed beads. Pass through the bead in Round 3 and pass through all 12 beads of the petal again. Repeat twice more to reinforce the petal. Pass through 2 beads in Round 3. Attach the link of etched cable chain to this petal.

3 String 12 size 11° seed beads and pass through 2 beads in Round 3 (Figure 3). Repeat twelve times to fill Round 3 with 14 petals. Weave the needle and thread through to Round 2.

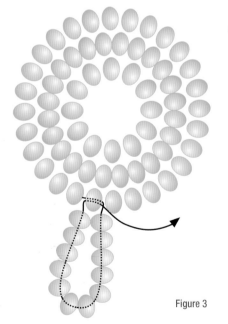

Figure 3

4 String 8 size 11° triangle beads and pass through 2 beads in Round 2 (Figure 4). Repeat eleven times to fill Round 2 with 12 petals. Weave the needle and thread through to Round 1.

Figure 4

5 String 1 magatama and pass through 2 beads in Round 1. Repeat eleven times to attach 12 magatamas to Round 1. Weave in thread ends, tying half-hitch knots between several beads, and trim.

6 Use the measuring tape to find the center of the flat oval chain. Use chain- and flat-nose pliers to open a link in the center of the chain and divide the chain into two 8" (20cm) pieces.

7 Use the link of etched cable chain to attach one end of each piece of flat oval chain to the reinforced petal of the flower.

8 Use one 4mm jump ring to attach the leaf toggle bar to the open end of one piece of flat oval chain. Use the other 4mm jump ring to attach the nouveau toggle ring to the open end of the other piece of flat oval chain.

Lampworking—A Centuries-Old Tradition

Lampworking (also called *flameworking*) is a technique that has changed little over the centuries. Originally named for the technique of working with thin glass rods over a hot oil lamp, today's lampwork artists use small propane torches to heat glass rods that, when molten, are wound around a *mandrel* (metal rod). The artist uses one hand to rotate the mandrel as the glass is wound in order to distribute the glass evenly. The glass rods can be layered to form a bead with colorful depths. They can also be used to decorate the bead's surface with dots, lines, and other textures.

After the bead is formed and decorated, the bead is placed in a hot kiln in order to cool slowly. This process, *annealing,* ensures that the bead will not become brittle from cooling too rapidly. Modern lampworkers create what are referred to as "art glass beads." The best of these can be viewed as miniature works of art and are usually designed by artists in individual studios. Their designs range from beads that incorporate forms from nature—flowers and pods, sea creatures, hearts, and more—to beads with a decided geometric or architectural bent. Many contemporary lampwork artists are also incorporating metal clay into the surface of their beads. Glass's protean qualities are ideal for such collectible creations.

Fig. 97. — Ouvrière parisienne soufflant une fausse perle.

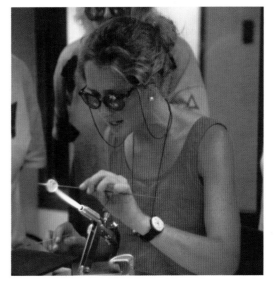

Compare the nineteenth-century French engraving of a female lampworker and the photograph of contemporary glass artist Kristina Logan to see that this glass-making technique has remained much the same over the decades. Engraving from the Collection of the Rakow Research Library of The Corning Museum of Glass, Corning, NY. Photograph from the Collection of The Corning Museum of Glass, Corning, NY, taken at The Studio of The Corning Museum of Glass.

Lotus Link

The lotus flower, which represents peace and serenity, is the focal point of this lovely necklace. Thai silver flowers in the form of head pins, rings, and clasp are enhanced by glass beads in the subtle colors of the charming flower. All components come together to form an enlightening piece of jewelry.

1 Use the wire of 1 young bloom head pin to connect 2 silver lotus rings: Hold the rings in your non-dominant hand and hold the head pin in your dominant hand. Place the head pin's flower up between the 2 rings. Wrap the length of the head pin's wire around both rings in a figure-eight motion. You should be able to form about three figure eights. Use chain-nose pliers to tuck the end of the head pin's wire. Repeat entire step to form a second set of lotus rings.

2 Attach one 6mm jump ring to the leaf half of the clasp. Use one 6mm jump ring to attach the previous jump ring to the single lotus ring. Attach two 6mm jump rings to the lotus ring. Attach one 6mm jump ring to the two previous jump rings. Use two 6mm jump rings to connect the previous jump ring to one side of one set of lotus rings. Use two 6mm jump rings to the other side of the set of lotus rings. Attach one 6mm jump ring to the two previous jump rings. Use two 6mm jump rings to connect the previous jump ring to one side of the other set of lotus rings.

3 Use 1 young bloom head pin to string 1 fire-polished round. Form a wrapped loop that attaches to the single jump ring used to connect the pairs of jump rings between lotus rings. Repeat to attach a second wrapped head pin to the same jump ring. Repeat entire step to attach 2 head pins to the single jump ring used to connect the pairs of jump rings between the other lotus rings.

4 Use 1 young bloom head pin to string 1 fire-polished round; form a wrapped loop. Repeat to make a second dangle. Attach the 3mm jump ring to the 2 wrapped loops. Use the 4mm jump ring to attach the 3mm jump ring to the middle lotus ring.

5 Use the 2" (5cm) head pin to string 1 fire-polished round, 1 Javanese lampworked round, the flower half of the clasp, 1 Javanese lampworked round, and 1 fire-polished round. Form a wrapped loop.

6 Use the beading wire to string 1 crimp tube, 10 seed beads, and the wrapped loop formed in Step 5. Pass back through the tube and crimp. Cover the tube with a crimp cover. String 1 seed bead, 1 fire-polished round, 1 Javanese lampworked round, and 1 Czech pressed-glass coin fifteen times. String 1 crimp tube, 10 seed beads, and the fifth link of the lotus flower chain. Pass back through the tube; crimp and cover.

did you know . . .

Glass as Art—The American Studio Glass Movement

In the 1950s, a ceramic artist named Peter Voulkos began breaking new and exciting ground with his pottery. His unique designs and glazes were abstract expressionist to the core, with energetic forms that the artist tore apart, rebuilt, and textured vigorously. Because of his revolutionary and painterly approach to this traditional craft, art critics and collectors began to see ceramics as an art form. Inspired by Voulkos's work, Harvey Littleton, a teaching ceramist at the University of Wisconsin in Madison, began parallel experiments in glass.

In America prior to the 1950s, virtually all glass objects were made in industrial environments. In fact, Littleton's own father was the head of Research and Development at the Corning Glassworks during the 1930s. After a visit to Murano, Italy, in the fifties, Littleton saw the possibilities for creating smaller-scale artist studios to make glass. There, he witnessed demonstrations by craftsmen (mostly for tourists), where small furnaces were staffed by only a couple of workers. After his return to the States, Littleton started experimenting with small batches of glass in his ceramics kiln. The early experiments led to his first major glassblowing workshop in 1962, sponsored by the Toledo Museum of Art. An essential partner in this enterprise was Dominick Labino, a glass research scientist who developed a small, affordable furnace in which to melt and work with glass. Littleton, credited as the father of the American studio glass movement, taught many disciples who went on to illustrious careers as glass artists—among them, Dale Chihuly, Fritz Dreisbach, and Marvin Lipofsky. Most of all, Littleton's pioneering work in glass elevated glass forms to fine art.

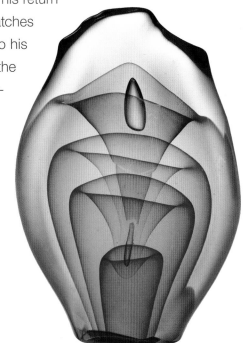

This glass sculpture, entitled *Emergence Four-Stage,* is by studio glass pioneer Dominick Labino (1975). Collection of The Corning Museum of Glass, Corning, NY, purchased with the aid of funds from the National Endowment for the Arts.

Venetian Vines

MATERIALS

17 green AB 3mm fire-polished rounds

10 dark green 3mm fire-polished rounds

10 aquamarine 3mm fire-polished rounds

4 teal and topaz 3x5mm fire-polished rondelles

30 teal and topaz 6x8mm Czech pressed-glass teardrops

5 teal and cream 6x8mm Czech pressed-glass leaves

6 aqua and gold-lined teal 14mm Venetian glass bicolor foil discs

5 dark aqua 16mm Venetian glass textured frit rounds

1 dark aqua 20mm Venetian glass textured frit round

1 aqua and gold-lined teal 23mm Venetian glass bicolor foil discs

2 vermeil 12x31mm leaf chandelier connectors

1 vermeil 10x25mm hook-and-eye clasp

4 gold-filled 2mm crimp tubes

4 gold-filled 3.4mm crimp covers

1 gold-filled 4mm jump ring

6" (15cm) of gold-filled 22-gauge half-hard wire

21" (53cm) of gold .019 beading wire

TOOLS

Wire cutters

Round-nose pliers

Chain-nose pliers

Flat-nose pliers

Crimping pliers

FINISHED SIZE

18" (46cm)

Two styles of gorgeous handmade Venetian beads are perfectly matched with Czech pressed-glass teardrops and leaves in this asymmetrical necklace. Gold vermeil leaf connectors and fire-polished rounds square-stitched to the teardrops give enough weight to visually balance the two sides of the necklace, while allowing the uniqueness of each type of bead to shine.

1 Use flat-nose pliers to form a 135° bend with the last 1½" (4cm) of the 6" (15cm) wire. String one green AB fire-polished round down to the bend. Wrap the short end of the wire around the bead and form a wrapped loop above the bead (Figure 1). Trim the short end of wire. Use the remaining wire to string the 23mm Venetian glass bicolor foil disc, 1 green AB fire-polished round, the 20mm Venetian glass textured frit round, 1 green AB fire-polished round. Form a double-wrapped loop that attaches to the loop end of one leaf chandelier connector.

Figure 1

2 Use 10" (25cm) of wire to string 1 crimp tube and the leaf end of the leaf chandelier connector. Pass back through the tube and crimp. Cover the tube with a crimp cover. String 1 green AB fire-polished round.

3 String 2 pressed-glass teardrops, 1 dark green fire-polished round, and 1 aquamarine fire-polished round. Pass through the last teardrop strung again (Figure 2). String 1 teardrop, 1 pressed-glass leaf, 2 teardrops, 1 aquamarine fire-polished round, and 1 dark green fire-polished round. Pass through the last teardrop strung again. String 1 teardrop and 1 fire-polished rondelle.

4 Repeat Step 3 three times, replacing the final rondelle with 1 green AB fire-polished round. String 1 crimp tube and the leaf end of the second leaf chandelier connector. Pass back through the tube; crimp and cover. Use the 4mm jump ring to attach the loop end of the chandelier connector to the hook half of the clasp.

5 Use 11" (28cm) of wire to string 1 crimp tube and the loop end of the first leaf chandelier connector. Pass back through the tube; crimp and cover. String 1 green AB fire-polished round, one 14mm Venetian glass bicolor foil disc, 1 green AB fire-polished round, and one 16mm Venetian glass textured frit round six times, omitting the final 16mm Venetian glass textured frit round. String 1 crimp tube and the eye half of the clasp. Pass back through the tube and crimp.

TINY GEMS

Glass has a long history of serving as a "fabulous fake" when it comes to jewelry. Ancient Egyptian glassmakers produced primarily opaque glass, often simulating favored gemstones turquoise, carnelian, and lapis lazuli. Later, in the seventeenth century, glass paste (made with molten glass that frequently had a high lead content) was developed to imitate precious stones.

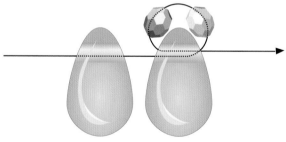

Figure 2

Dharma Wheel

MATERIALS

About 5 g of waterfall size 15° seed
    beads

About 10 g of waterfall size 11° seed
    beads (A)

About 5 g of mint-lined aqua size 11°
    seed beads (B)

About 5 g of spearmint size 11° seed
    beads (C)

About 5 g of buckskin size 11° seed
    beads (D)

About 5 g of amber yellow size 11°
    seed beads (E)

1 mottled teal 8mm Czech pressed-
    glass bead

2 yellow 6x8mm Czech pressed-glass
    faceted ovals

3 teal and topaz 8x10mm Czech
    pressed-glass faceted round

2 mottled teal 8x14mm Czech pressed-
    glass curved rectangles

2 cherry wood 20mm spiral flower link

1 cherry wood 40mm spiral flower
    pendant

1 natural brass tiny hook-and-eye
    clasp

2 natural brass 8mm jump rings

5½" (14cm) of ¼" (.64cm) wide
    Terrifically Tacky Tape

Yellow size D, 6lb test FireLine braided
    beading thread

TOOLS

Scissors

Size 10 beading needle

Chain-nose pliers

Flat-nose pliers (or second pair of
    chain-nose pliers)

FINISHED SIZE

7" (18cm)

The Dharma Wheel is an eight-spoked Buddhist symbol representing the natural and moral principles that apply to all beings. With its eight petals, the spiral flower pendant used is a stylized version of this teaching and, along with the smooth flow of seed-bead colors, is a fashionable way to remind us always to do the right thing.

1 Use single-needle ladder stitch to form a chain of 6A beads, leaving a 16" (41cm) tail thread.

2 Use herringbone stitch to form the base of the bracelet:

Row 1: With the thread exiting the bead on one end of the ladder-stitch chain, string 2A and pass down through the second bead in the chain. Pass up through the third bead in the chain. String 2A and pass down through the fourth bead in the chain. Pass up through the fifth bead in the chain. String 2A and pass down through the sixth bead in the chain (Figure 1).

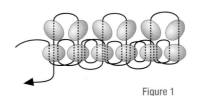

Figure 1

Row 2: Weave through beads so that you are exiting the last bead strung in the previous row. *String 2A, pass down through the bead in the previous row and up through the next bead in the same row. Repeat from * twice.

Rows 3–7: Repeat Row 2.

Rows 8–12: Repeat Row 2 for each row, fading from A beads to B beads by randomly replacing 1A with 1B in Row 8, 2A with 2B in Row 9, 3A with 3B in Row 10, 4A with 4B in Row 11, and 5A with 5B in Row 12.

Row 13: Repeat Row 2 using B beads.

Rows 14–18: Repeat as for Rows 8–12, fading from B beads to C beads.

Row 19: Repeat Row 2 using C beads.

Rows 20–24: Repeat as for Rows 8–12, fading from C beads to A beads.

Row 25: Repeat Row 2.

Rows 26–30: Repeat as for Rows 8–12, fading from A beads to D beads.

Row 31: Repeat Row 2 using D beads.

Rows 32–37: Repeat as for Rows 8–12, fading from D beads to E beads.

Row 38: Repeat Row 2 using E beads.

Rows 39–43: Repeat as for Rows 8–12, fading from E beads to A beads.

Rows 44–49: Repeat Row 2, using A beads for every row.

Rows 50–54: Repeat Rows 8–12.

Row 55: Repeat Row 13.

Rows 56–60: Repeat Rows 14–18.

Row 61: Repeat Row 19.

Rows 62–66: Repeat Rows 20–24.

Rows 67–72: Repeat Rows 44–49.

Rows 73–77: Repeat Rows 26–30.

Row 78: Repeat Row 31.

Rows 79–82: Repeat as for Rows 8–12, fading from D beads to E beads.

Row 83: Repeat Row 38.

Rows 84–88: Repeat Rows 39–43.

Rows 89–98: Repeat Row 2, using A beads for every row.

3 Use the remaining working thread to weave through beads and exit the third bead in Row 98. String 1A, the hook half of the clasp, one 8mm jump ring, one hole of one wood link, 1A, and 1 size 15° seed bead. Pass back through the A, link, jump ring, and A. Pass through the fourth bead in Row 98. Weave through beads and stitch through all of the beads used in this step again to reinforce.

4 Weave thread through to exit the third bead in Row 89. String 1A, the other hole of the link, 1A, and 1 size 15° seed bead. Pass back through the A, link, and A. Pass through the fourth bead in Row 89. Weave through beads and stitch through all of the beads used in this step again to reinforce.

5 Use the tail thread to repeat Step 3 on the other end of the bracelet (Row 1), using the eye half of the clasp and omitting the jump ring. Repeat Step 4, attaching the link to Row 11.

6 Secure a new thread and weave to the first bead in Row 21. String 3 size 15°s, 1 glass round, and 3 size 15°s. Pass through the sixth bead in Row 21. String 3 size 15°s and pass through the glass round. String 3 size 15°s and pass through the first bead in Row 21. Pass through all beads again to reinforce.

7 Repeat Step 6 at Row 35, replacing the glass round with 1 glass oval.

8 Repeat Step 6 at Row 46.

9 Repeat Step 6 at Row 58, replacing the glass round with 1 glass square.

10 Repeat Step 6 at Row 69.

11 Repeat Step 6 at Row 79, replacing the glass round with 1 glass oval.

12 Attach one 8mm jump ring to the bail of the wood pendant. Remove one side of the Tacky Tape backing of a 5" (13cm) piece of tape. Stick one end of the tape to the pendant on one side of the bail. Wrap the tape around the circumference of the pendant.

TINY GEMS

Glass beads were interred with the dead in ancient times to serve as a talisman in the afterlife. Greater quantities of beads and more elaborately wrought beads signified a royal or noble person.

13 Thread the needle with a comfortable length of thread. Stick the last 1" (2.5cm) of thread to the tape on one side of the bail (you may need to keep pressing the thread end into the tape until it is covered with beads and the tape has cured). String 82A and carefully place them on the tape around the circumference of the pendant.

14 When you reach the other side of the bail, string 2A. Pass back through the last 2A strung in Step 13 and pass through the 2A just strung. *String 5A, place them on the tape on the edge of the pendant, and pass back through 2A from Step 13. Repeat from * around the pendant, stringing 5 or 6A and passing back through 2A to secure, to add a total of 85 beads to this row. Repeat entire step on the other side of the beads strung in Step 13.

15 Repeat Step 14 on each side of the pendant adding about 72A to each side. Weave in thread ends and trim.

16 Attach ¼" (.64cm) of tape to the center of one side of the pendant. Attach 1 glass curved rectangle to the tape. Repeat on the other side of the pendant.

MATERIALS

About 5 g medium turquoise pastel
   size 15° seed beads

About 5 g red size 15° seed beads

15 bracken yellow size 15° seed beads

10 yellow with dots 6mm Javanese
   lampworked glass rounds

10 teal with yellow dots 4x8mm
   Javanese lampworked glass
   rondelles

10 yellow with red waves 5x10mm
   Javanese lampworked glass tubes

6 red with teal and yellow dots 10mm
   Javanese lampworked glass rounds

5 red and white 15mm Venetian lampworked glass mosaic squares

5 sterling silver 7x10mm petal charms

1 sterling silver 16mm Corazon box
   clasp

4 sterling silver 2mm crimp tubes

2 sterling silver 3.4mm crimp covers

19" (48cm) of .019 beading wire

Clear size D, 6lb test FireLine braided
   beading thread

TOOLS

Wire cutters

Crimping pliers

Bead stop

Scissors

Size 13 beading needle

Thread burner

FINISHED SIZE

15¼" (39cm)

Bright Amulet

This bracelet proves you really can blend patterns, just as long as you choose beads in the same color palette—in this case red, turquoise, and yellow. Simple stringing embellished with tiny seed beads and silver charms results in a wonderfully textured piece. When you have this colorful bracelet wrapped twice around your wrist, you'll have all the protection you need.

1 Use the beading wire to string 2 crimp tubes and one half of the clasp. Pass back through the tubes and crimp, leaving about 1mm of bare wire between the tubes. Cover the tube closest to the clasp with a crimp cover. String 1 red with teal and yellow dots 10mm Javanese lampworked glass round.

2 String 1 yellow with red waves 5×10mm Javanese lampworked glass tube, 1 teal with yellow dots 4×8mm Javanese lampworked glass rondelle, 1 yellow with dots 6mm Javanese lampworked glass round, 1 red and white 15mm Venetian lampworked glass mosaic square, 1 yellow with dots 6mm Javanese lampworked glass round, 1 teal with yellow dots 4×8mm Javanese lampworked glass rondelle, 1 yellow with red waves 5×10mm Javanese lampworked glass tube, and 1 red with teal and yellow dots 10mm Javanese lampworked glass round five times. String 2 crimp tubes and the other half of the clasp. Place the bead stop on the wire about ¼" (.64cm) from the last bead strung.

3 Use the needle to string a long, comfortable length of braided beading thread. Tie the thread between the 2 crimp tubes using a surgeon's knot and leaving an 8" (20cm) tail thread. Pass through the red glass round.

4 String 14 red size 15° seed beads and pass through the teal glass rondelle. String 10 red size 15° seed beads and pass through the Venetian glass mosaic square. String 10 red size 15° seed beads and pass through the teal glass rondelle. String 14 red size 15° seed beads and pass through the red glass round.

5 Repeat Step 4 four times. Pass through 1 crimp tube. Tie a square knot and pass back through the tube, making sure to leave enough slack in the thread so that the knot does not follow back through the tube. Pass back through the red glass round.

6 Repeat Step 4 five times, using medium turquoise pastel size 15° seed beads, passing back through all of the beads and toward the other end of the clasp, and stopping before passing back through the final red glass round. Pass the thread through the yellow glass tube, the teal glass rondelle, and the yellow glass round.

7 String 3 red size 15°s, 3 medium turquoise pastel size 15°s, 1 bracken yellow size 15°, 1 petal charm, and 1 bracken yellow size 15°. Pass back through the petal charm and string 1 bracken yellow size 15°, 3 medium turquoise pastel size 15°s, and 3 red size 15°s.

8 Pass through all of the Javanese glass beads until you reach the next Venetian glass mosaic square. Repeat Step 7.

9 Repeat Step 8 three times. Pass through glass beads until you reach the end of the bracelet. Pass through the first crimp tube and tie a surgeon's knot around the wire between the two beads. Pass back through the crimp tube.

TINY GEMS

In the eighteenth and nineteenth centuries, the indigenous Ainu people of Japan prized glass-bead necklaces. They made their necklaces from beads obtained from China or mainland Japan—most often blue, black, or white. Additionally, a wooden medallion decorated with metal rosettes was sometimes added. Ainu women wore the necklaces on formal occasions.

10 Remove the bead stop. Snug the beads, leaving enough slack so that the bracelet will wrap twice around your wrist, and crimp the tubes. Place a crimp cover on the tube closest to the clasp.

11 Use the needle and thread to pass back through a bead and tie an overhand knot a few times to secure. Trim thread and burn end. Repeat using the tail thread.

fashion-forward

When you bought a ticket to the local design school's annual fashion show, you weren't at all sure you'd actually attend. Wasn't it enough to make a donation by buying the ticket? Good thing you didn't miss out on this event because, ever since the lights dimmed and young models began gliding down the runway in student clothing designs, you've been transfixed. What color, what layering and texture, what fun! Is plaid really going to dominate fashion trends? Will boots be both sleek and slouchy, but most of all a power accessory? Are women of all ages going to wear embellished tunics?

Forget about ready-made clothes, you think. Seeing these fresh, sassy, innovative styles has inspired you. You long to add personal, original touches to your wardrobe. And while you know you don't have a couture budget, you do know you love to make things by hand—especially jewelry.

An evening of **Fashion-Forward** styles might have you dreaming of creating a dramatic bracelet with tribal-looking matte-glass dangles and earthy beads. Or it could take you directly to a brass chain necklace with jadelike glass beads and a scarab pendant, reminiscent of art nouveau, but updated for a trendier look. Then again, you might be up for blue glass beads and big stars that add up to earrings that make you feel as daring as Wonder Woman!

MATERIALS

About 7 g chartreuse size 11° seed
beads

About 3 g golden mineral red size 11°
seed beads

36 matte gold antiqued amber 12mm
twist bugle beads

24 mottled chartreuse 4mm fire-
polished rounds

2 lime-green 14mm Venetian lampworked glass rounds

4 lime-green-stamped brown 9x14mm
lampworked glass rondelles

1 green-and-brown 18x30mm lampworked glass acorn focal bead

2 gold-filled 14mm round components

2 gold-filled 20mm round components

1 gold vermeil 18mm toggle clasp

12 gold-filled 2mm crimp tubes

12 gold-filled 3.4mm crimp covers

8 gold-filled 6mm jump rings

1 gold-filled 20-gauge 3" (8cm) head
pin

10" (25cm) of gold-filled 20-gauge
half-hard wire

96" (244cm) of butterscotch .014
beading wire

TOOLS

Wire cutters

Flat-nose pliers

Chain-nose pliers

Round-nose pliers

Crimping pliers

FINISHED SIZE

19¼" (49cm)

Romancing the Acorn

The organic flow and feel of this necklace stem from the stunning glass acorn handmade by Joyce Rooks. Its colors are echoed in lampworked rondelles, Venetian glass rounds, and several strands of strung seed beads. The gold components give the piece a light and airy feel, while the star of the necklace—the acorn—lends a bit of whimsical romance.

1 Use the head pin to string 1 fire-polished round, the acorn bead, and 1 fire-polished round. Form a wrapped loop that attaches to both of the 20mm round components.

2 Use 5" (13cm) of 20-gauge wire to form a wrapped loop that attaches to both of the 20mm round components. String 1 fire-polished round, 1 lampworked glass rondelle, 1 Venetian glass round, 1 lampworked glass rondelle, and 1 fire-polished round. Form a wrapped loop that attaches to one 14mm round component.

3 Use 16" (41cm) of wire to string the 14mm round component. Use both ends of the wire to string 1 fire-polished round.

4 Use one end of the wire to string 21 chartreuse size 11° seed beads. String 1 twist bugle bead and 1 chartreuse size 11° three times. String 20 chartreuse size 11°s, 21 golden mineral red size 11° seed beads, 10 chartreuse size 11°s, 1 fire-polished round, 1 crimp tube, and 1 jump ring. Pass back through the tube and crimp. Cover the tube with a crimp cover.

5 Repeat Step 4 using the other end of wire, and using the same jump ring as in Step 4.

6 Repeat Steps 3–5 twice.

7 Use 1 jump ring to attach the 3 jump rings at the ends of the strands of beads to one half of the clasp.

8 Repeat Steps 2–7 for the other half of the necklace.

TINY GEMS

While he is usually credited with originating the formula for leaded glass, English entrepreneur George Ravenscroft likely received the formula from a Venetian glassmaker he had hired, Giacomo da Costa. Ravenscroft patented the formula in the late seventeenth century, thus securing his reputation as the inventor of leaded glass.

did you know . . .

The Bohemian Revolution, 1820–1935

As early as the thirteenth century, Bohemia (today part of the Czech Republic) made glass. But the real golden age of Bohemian glass began in the early eighteenth century, when the somewhat-isolated region began to trade throughout Europe and beyond. The export of glass became integral to the economy of the region. Thus, the Napoleonic wars had a devastating effect on the industry, and it took more than a decade afterward for Bohemia to recover. Both glass factories and independent glass decorators contributed to keeping the region strong in both artistry and technology.

While Bohemian glass beadmakers learned much from the Venetian artisans, often reproducing their distinctive forms such as millefiori and chevron beads, they had their own innovations. They excelled in creating pressed-glass beads (beads made in molds), faceting glass beads as if they were gems, and imitating gemstones and pearls. They also gained a worldwide reputation for cut glassware with elaborate carved patterning. Such innovations were frequently copied by rivals, who often stooped to breaking into the workshops of some of the leading glass artists to steal their secrets. One famous nineteenth-century Bohemian glassmaker, Daniel Swarovski, moved his entire crystal-cutting operation to Austria in order to foil rivals looking to steal his patented machine-cutting process.

Many of today's beautiful Czech glass beads and buttons are made by some of the same glass factories and families, using some of the same molds that were popular in the 1920s through 1930s.

This blown-glass Bohemian vase (circa 1830), from the workshop of famous glassmaker Friedrich Egermann (1777–1864), is made of lithyalin, a type of glass he developed that is opaque, with a marbled glass surface resembling semiprecious stones. Collection of The Corning Museum of Glass, Corning, NY.

Sweet Treat

MATERIALS

About 80 red-lined light lime size 11°
  seed beads

8 orange 4x6mm fire-polished glass
  rondelles

8 orange 6mm fire-polished glass
  rounds

6 mottled orange 6x8mm Czech
  pressed-glass rounds

4 mottled orange 10mm Czech
  pressed-glass squares

2 orange 8x35mm Venetian glass
  curved tubes

6 black silver 7mm spiral wrap coil
  beads

8 black silver 6x12mm little flower
  cluster charms

1 black silver 14mm toggle clasp with
  jump ring

4 black silver 2mm crimp tubes

22 silver 2" (5cm) head pins

10" (25cm) of black .019 beading
  wire

TOOLS

Chain-nose pliers

Flat-nose pliers

Round-nose pliers

Wire cutters

Crimping pliers

FINISHED SIZE

8" (20cm)

Only two bright orange Venetian-glass curved tubes are needed to make this bracelet look like a delectable treat. The tubes curve nicely around your wrist and, with a center full of charms and wire-wrapped pressed-glass beads, this bracelet is definitely a piece of yummy eye candy.

1 Use 1 head pin to string 1 seed bead, one 4×6mm rondelle, and 1 seed bead. Form a wrapped loop. Repeat entire step three times for a total of four 4×6mm rondelle dangles.

2 Use 1 head pin to string 1 seed bead, one 6mm round, and 1 seed bead. Form a wrapped loop. Repeat entire step three times for a total of 4 round dangles.

3 Use 1 head pin to string one 4×6mm rondelle, 1 seed bead, and one 6mm round. Form a wrapped loop. Repeat entire step three times for a total of 4 mixed dangles.

4 Use 1 head pin to string 1 seed bead, one 6×8mm rondelle, and 1 seed bead. Form a wrapped loop. Repeat entire step three times for a total of four 6×8mm round dangles.

5 Use 1 head pin to string 1 seed bead, one 10mm square, and 1 seed bead. Form a wrapped loop. Repeat entire step three times for a total of 4 square dangles.

6 Use 1 head pin to string 1 seed bead, one 6mm black silver coil bead, and 1 seed bead. Form a wrapped loop. Repeat entire step once for a total of 2 coil dangles.

7 Use the beading wire to string 2 crimp tubes and one half of the clasp. Pass back through the crimp tubes and crimp. String 1 seed bead, one 6×8mm rondelle, 1 seed bead, 1 black silver coil bead, 1 seed bead, 1 curved tube, 1 seed bead, and 1 black silver coil bead.

8 String 1 seed bead, one 4×6mm rondelle dangle, 1 cluster charm, 1 seed bead, 1 mixed dangle, 1 seed bead, one 6×8mm rondelle dangle, 1 cluster charm, 1 seed bead, 1 round dangle, 1 seed bead, 1 square dangle, 1 cluster charm, 1 seed bead, one 4×6mm rondelle, 1 seed bead, 1 coil dangle, 1 seed bead, 1 mixed dangle, 1 seed bead, 1 square dangle, 1 cluster charm, 1 seed bead, 1 round dangle, 1 seed bead, one 6×8mm rondelle charm, 1 seed bead, 1 cluster charm, 1 mixed dangle, 1 seed bead, 1 square dangle, 1 cluster charm, 1 seed bead, 1 round dangle, 1 seed bead, one 6×8mm rondelle dangle, 1 seed bead, 1 coil dangle, 1 seed bead, one 4×6mm rondelle dangle, 1 seed bead, 1 cluster charm, 1 square dangle, 1 seed bead, 1 round dangle, 1 cluster charm, 1 seed bead, one 6×8mm rondelle dangle, 1 seed bead, 1 mixed dangle, 1 seed bead, 1 cluster charm, one 4×6mm rondelle dangle, and 1 seed bead.

9 Repeat Step 7, reversing the stringing sequence and attaching the wire to the other half of the clasp.

TINY GEMS

Artisans from ancient Rome made elaborately carved glass cameos. A dark-colored glass (usually blue) was cased with opaque white glass to form the cameo blank. The artisan then carved a relief pattern into the layered glass. Using glass instead of shell or stone gave the artisan greater control over the depth and placement of the contrasting layers.

Wonder Woman

MATERIALS

About 5 g spectrum blue size 11° seed
    beads

2 cobalt blue/red/white 8mm glass
    chevron rounds

4 sterling silver 4mm faceted rounds

2 sterling silver 7x10mm oval
    components

2 sterling silver 25mm star
    components

2 sterling silver 40x50mm teardrop
    components

1 pair sterling silver ear wires

6" (15cm) of sterling silver 22-gauge
    half-hard wire

240" (610cm) of non-tarnish silver
    26-gauge wire

TOOLS

Wire cutters

Chain-nose pliers

Flat-nose pliers

Round-nose pliers

FINISHED SIZE

3½" (9cm)

Sure, she had her cuffs, but couldn't our superheroine use some earrings, too? If she did want to add more accessories, these earrings would be perfect! Sterling silver components wire wrapped with blue seed beads are topped off with chevrons, resulting in a powerful pair of earrings.

1 Hold the last 1½" (4cm) of one end of 120" (305cm) of 26-gauge wire against 1 teardrop component. Wrap the wire twice around the component, securing the tail end of wire (Figure 1).

Figure 1

Figure 2

Figure 3

2 String 3 seed beads and wrap the wire around the component, making sure the middle bead sits on the outside edge of the component (Figure 2).

3 Repeat Step 2 fourteen times.

4 Use your non-dominant hand to hold 1 star component in the center of the teardrop component. String 3 seed beads. Wrap the wire through the component and around the teardrop—there will be about ⅛" (.32cm) of wire showing between the star and the teardrop (Figure 3).

5 Repeat Step 2 thirty times.

6 Repeat Step 4 on the other side of the components.

7 Repeat Step 2 fifteen times.

8 Wrap the wire all around the teardrop component again, placing each round of wire between rounds of beads. Secure the end of the wire by wrapping it around the top of the teardrop several times. Hide the wire end at the top of the teardrop.

9 Use 3" (8cm) of 22-gauge wire to form a 6mm wrapped loop that attaches to the top of the teardrop component, looping around the beads and wire. String 1 silver faceted round, 1 chevron, and 1 silver faceted round. Form a wrapped loop that attaches to 1 oval component.

10 Attach 1 ear wire to the oval component.

11 Repeat Steps 1–10 for the second earring.

TINY GEMS

Faience, a ceramic similar in composition to glass, was used extensively in Egypt for beadmaking. At banquets in ancient Egypt, honored guests were frequently presented with faience bead collars as party favors.

Tribal Relics

MATERIALS

16 silvery aspen size 11° seed beads

12 shimmering shadow lined size 8°
seed beads

2 topaz 4mm fire-polished rounds

7 mottled topaz 4x6mm Czech
pressed-glass rondelles

4 mottled brown 8mm Czech pressed-
glass bicones

2 mottled cream-and-brown 6x15mm
Czech pressed-glass bamboo tubes

4 black 9x18mm Czech pressed-glass
arrowheads

4 sterling silver 10x5mm square cord
ends

1 sterling silver 18mm rectangle toggle
clasp

5 sterling silver 4mm jump rings

1 sterling silver 8mm jump ring

5 sterling silver 9mm jump rings

4 sterling silver 2mm crimp tubes

4 sterling silver 3.4mm crimp covers

18" (46cm) of sterling silver 22-gauge
dead-soft wire

11" (28cm) of silver .019 beading wire

7" (18cm) of black 3mm braided
leather cord

Beacon's 3-in-1 advanced craft glue

TOOLS

Wire cutters

Crimping pliers

Chain-nose pliers

Flat-nose pliers

Round-nose pliers

FINISHED SIZE

7½" (19cm)

Though not actually artifacts from the past, the parts and pieces that compose this bracelet give off an antique vibe. Charms formed of pressed-glass arrowheads connect the two strands made of vintage-looking glass beads and braided leather cord for a bracelet that will surely survive the ages.

1 Cut the leather cord in half. Use the glue to attach 1 cord end to each end of the leather cords. Let dry.

2 Use 3" (8cm) of 22-gauge wire to form a double-wrapped loop. String 1 size 11° seed bead, 1 pressed-glass rondelle, and 1 size 11° seed bead. Form a double-wrapped loop that attaches to one 4mm jump ring. Use one 4mm jump ring to attach the previous jump ring to the bar half of the clasp. Use one 4mm jump ring to attach the remaining wrapped loop to the loop of 1 cord end on one piece of leather. Set aside.

3 Use 5½" (14cm) of .019 beading wire to string 1 crimp tube and the loop of 1 cord end on the second piece of leather. Pass back through the tube and crimp. Cover the tube with a crimp cover.

4 String 1 size 11° seed bead, 1 pressed-glass bicone, 1 size 11° seed bead, 1 pressed-glass rondelle, 1 size 11° seed bead, 1 pressed-glass bamboo tube, 1 size 11° seed bead, 1 pressed-glass rondelle, 1 size 11° seed bead, 1 pressed-glass bicone, and 1 size 11° seed bead.

5 String 1 crimp tube and the last 4mm jump ring used in Step 2. Pass back through the tube; crimp and cover. Use one 4mm jump ring to attach the loop of the cord end on the other end of the leather to the ring half of the clasp.

6 Use a crimp tube to attach 5½" (14cm) of .019 beading wire to the jump ring attached to the ring half of the clasp. Cover the tube with a crimp cover. Repeat Step 4. String 1 crimp tube and the loop of the cord end set aside from Step 2. Pass back through the tube; crimp and cover.

7 Use 4" (10cm) of 22-gauge wire to form a double-wrapped loop. String 1 fire-polished round and form a 6mm double-wrapped loop that attaches to 1 pressed-glass arrowhead. Repeat to form a second fire-polished bead dangle.

8 Repeat Step 7, replacing the fire-polished round with a pressed-glass rondelle and making only one of this type of dangle.

9 Form the bracelet so that the two strands sit together; there should be about a 1½" section where the two leather pieces overlap.

10 Use chain- and flat-nose pliers to open one 9mm jump ring. String one of the dangles formed in Step 7 and close the jump ring around both pieces of leather.

11 Open one 9mm jump ring; string 6 size 8° seed beads and close the ring around both pieces of leather.

12 Repeat Step 10 using the dangle formed in Step 8. Repeat Step 11. Repeat Step 10.

13 Use 3" (8cm) of 22-gauge wire to form a double-wrapped loop that attaches to one 4mm jump ring. String 1 size 11° seed bead, 1 pressed-glass rondelle, and 1 size 11° seed bead. Form a double-wrapped loop that attaches to the 8mm jump ring. Attach the 8mm jump ring to 1 pressed-glass arrowhead. Attach the 4mm jump ring to the ring half of the clasp.

TINY GEMS

Ancient Roman glass, sought by collectors today, is often valued for its opalescent look. This iridescence was not created by the original glassmakers but is the effect of devitrification (chemical decomposition) over time, caused by contact with moisture and acidic soil.

Come to My Party

MATERIALS

5 g coral opaque luster size 11° seed
beads (A)

5 g salmon rose silver-lined size 11°
seed beads (B)

10 g rosy topaz matte silver-lined size
11° seed beads (C)

5 g rusty orange lined size 11° seed
beads (D)

5 g rusty orange lined size 8° seed
beads (E)

10 g dusty-coral-lined clear size 8°
seed beads (F)

16 orange 7mm Czech pressed-glass
flowers

16 orange 7x10mm Czech pressed-
glass "tongues"

8 orange 4x14mm Czech pressed-glass
daggers

12 orange/clear swirled 6x10mm
Czech pressed-glass rectangles

12 cream with orange and pink dots
18mm Venetian lampworked glass
beads

24 sterling silver 8mm flower bead
caps

1 sterling silver 15mm orange sequined
box clasp

22" (56cm) of .024 beading wire

Orange size D Nymo beading thread

TOOLS

Scissors

Size 11 beading needle

Wire cutters

Crimping pliers

FINISHED SIZE

18½" (47cm)

Bright orange Czech pressed-glass beads in three different shapes are stitched into a playful focal bead that is accented with polka-dotted Venetian lampworked glass and a sparkly sequined box clasp. Joyful colors and a blend of fun materials come together in a necklace that will invite people to take notice!

1 Use ladder stitch and size 8° seed beads to create a foundation chain 8 beads long. Connect the ends of the chain to form a tube, being careful not to twist the chain.

2 Use brick stitch to form a tube 9 rows long:

Row 1: String 1 size 8° seed bead and pass through the closest exposed loop of the foundation row. Pass back through the seed bead. Continue around, adding one bead at a time.

Rows 2–9: Repeat Row 1.

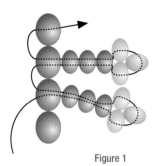

Figure 1

3 Add fringe to the brick stitch tube:

Row 1: With thread exiting the top of one of the beads in the first row, string 3C, 1B, 1A, and 1B. Pass back through the 3C. Pass down through the bead in the brick-stitch tube and up through the next bead in the tube. String 3D, 1A, 1B, and 1A. Pass back through the 3D. Pass down through the bead in the brick-stitch tube and up through the next bead in the tube. Repeat entire step around the tube (Figure 1).

Row 2: Repeat Row 1 around the tube, with the thread exiting the top of one of the beads in the second row. With thread exiting the top of one of the beads in the same row, string 1E, 1 flower, and 1C. Pass back through the flower and the E. Pass down through the bead in the tube and up through the next bead in the tube. Repeat entire step around the second row of the tube.

Row 3: With thread exiting the top of one of the beads in the third row, string 1E, 2C, 1B, 1A, and 1B. Pass back through the 2C and the E. Pass down through the bead in the tube and up through the next bead in the tube. Repeat entire step around the third row of the tube.

Row 4: With thread exiting the top of one of the beads in the fourth row, string 2C, 1 tongue, and 2C. Pass down through the bead in the tube and up through the next bead in the tube. Repeat entire step around the fourth row of the tube.

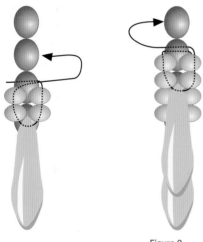
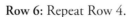

Figure 2

Row 5: With thread exiting the top of one of the beads in the fifth row, string 2C, 1 dagger, and 2C. Pass up through the bottom of the bead in the tube and down through the next bead in the tube. String 2C, 1 dagger, and 2C. Pass down through the bead in the tube and up through the next bead in the tube. Repeat entire step around the fifth row of the tube (Figure 2).

Row 6: Repeat Row 4.

Row 7: Repeat Row 3.

Row 8: Repeat Row 2.

Row 9: Repeat Row 1.

4 Use the beading wire to string 1 crimp tube, 1 size 8° seed bead, 9 coral opaque luster size 11° seed beads and one half of the clasp. Pass back through the size 8° and the tube. Crimp the tube and cover with a crimp cover.

5 String 1 size 8° seed bead, 1 bead cap, 1 Venetian glass bead, 1 bead cap, 1 size 8° seed bead, and 1 Czech pressed-glass rectangle six times.

6 String the focal piece formed in Steps 1–3.

7 String 1 Czech pressed-glass rectangle, 1 size 8° seed bead, 1 bead cap, 1 Venetian-glass bead, 1 bead cap, and 1 size 8° seed bead six times.

8 Repeat Step 1, attaching the wire to the other half of the clasp.

MATERIALS

About 5 g amber/rust matte lined
    size 11° seed beads

About 5 g amber white lined size 11°
    seed beads

About 5 g lemon-lime opaque size 11°
    seed beads

About 5 g light olive matte metallic size
    11° seed beads

About 5 g chartreuse matte size 11°
    seed beads

About 5 g light yellow-green matte
    metallic iris size 11° seed beads

About 5 g olive opaque size 11° seed
    beads

About 5 g olive matte size 11° seed
    beads

About 5 g dark purple lined size 11°
    seed beads

About 5 g grape transparent size 11°
    seed beads

About 5 g alexandrite matte lined size
    11° seed beads

About 5 g fuchsia matte lined size 11°
    seed beads

32 light olivine/bronze lined AB size 8°
    seed beads

5 assorted orange, yellow, red, purple,
    dark pink, and brown 16–30mm
    lampworked glass beads

1 gold-filled 23mm toggle clasp

2 gold-filled 2mm crimp tubes

2 gold-filled 3.4mm crimp covers

11" (28cm) of antique brass .024
    beading wire

Crystal clear size D, 6lb test FireLine
    braided beading thread

TOOLS

Scissors

Size 12 beading needle

Thread burner

Wire cutters

Crimping pliers

FINISHED SIZE

Size: 8" (21cm)

Rhumba

Twelve colors of peyote-stitched seed-bead discs pay tribute to beadmaker Sarah Moran, who used these colors when making this set of lampworked glass beads. Cheerful colors and the visual movement of the seed beads put one in the mood to dance. With its ruffles and sassy colors, this sumptuous bracelet is really just a celebration of the beads!

1 Use 1 color of size 11° seed beads and flat peyote stitch to form a disc:

Rounds 1 and 2: String 10 seed beads. Pass through the beads again to form a circle. Tie an overhand knot. Pass through 1 bead.

Round 3: String 2 seed beads. Skip 1 bead (in Round 1) and pass through 1 bead (in Round 2). Repeat around with the thread exiting the first bead of this round (Figure 1).

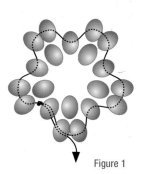

Figure 1

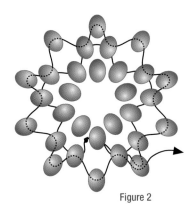

Figure 2

Round 4: String 1 seed bead. Pass through 1 bead in the previous round. Repeat around with the thread exiting the first bead of this round (Figure 2).

Round 5: Repeat Round 3.

Round 6: Repeat Round 4. Weave in thread ends, knotting between several beads, and trim ends with thread burner.

2 Repeat Step 1 twenty-three times, making two discs of each color of seed bead.

3 Use the beading wire to string 1 crimp tube and the ring half of the clasp. Pass back through the tube and crimp. Cover the tube with a crimp cover.

4 String 1 size 8° seed bead, 1 light olive matte metallic disc, 1 size 8° seed bead, 1 fuchsia matte lined disc, 1 size 8° seed bead, 1 olive opaque disc, 1 size 8° seed bead, 1 alexandrite matte lined disc, 1 size 8° seed bead, 1 lampworked glass bead, 1 size 8° seed bead, 1 olive matte disc, 1 size 8° seed bead, 1 amber/white lined disc, 1 size 8° seed bead, 1 light olive matte metallic disc, 1 size 8° seed bead, 1 dark purple lined, 1 size 8° seed bead, 1 lampworked glass bead, 1 size 8° seed bead, 1 chartreuse matte disc, 1 size 8° seed bead, 1 grape transparent disc, 1 size 8° seed bead, 1 amber/rust matte lined disc, 1 size 8° seed bead, 1 light yellow-green matte metallic iris disc, 1 size 8° seed bead, 1 lampworked glass bead, 1 lemon-lime opaque disc, 1 size 8° seed bead, 1 amber/rust matte lined disc, 1 size 8° seed bead, 1 dark purple lined disc, 1 size 8° seed bead, 1 olive matte disc, 1 size 8° seed bead,

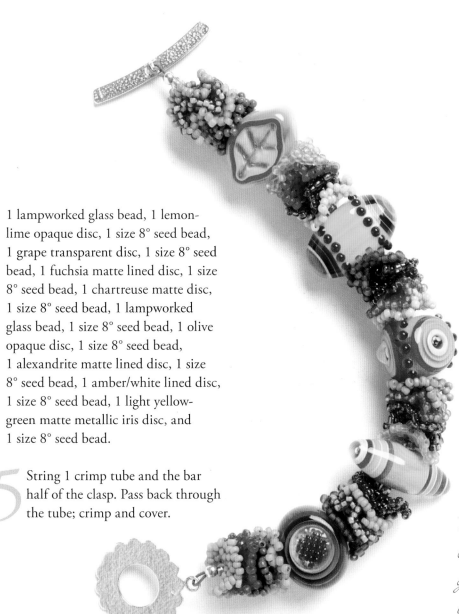

1 lampworked glass bead, 1 lemon-lime opaque disc, 1 size 8° seed bead, 1 grape transparent disc, 1 size 8° seed bead, 1 fuchsia matte lined disc, 1 size 8° seed bead, 1 chartreuse matte disc, 1 size 8° seed bead, 1 lampworked glass bead, 1 size 8° seed bead, 1 olive opaque disc, 1 size 8° seed bead, 1 alexandrite matte lined disc, 1 size 8° seed bead, 1 amber/white lined disc, 1 size 8° seed bead, 1 light yellow-green matte metallic iris disc, and 1 size 8° seed bead.

5 String 1 crimp tube and the bar half of the clasp. Pass back through the tube; crimp and cover.

TINY GEMS

Uranium glass, typically yellow or yellowish-green in color, originated in the early nineteenth century. Its distinctive color derived from uranium oxide.

Le Beau Jardin

MATERIALS

18 plum 6mm fire-polished glass
    rounds
10 green 8x14mm Czech pressed-glass
    leaves
4 hop green 5x10mm lampworked
    glass rondelles
1 hop green 18x35mm lampworked
    glass beetle
2 natural brass 16x20mm filigree leaf
    connectors
14 natural brass 3x8mm rondelles
1 natural brass 8mm lobster clasp
About 10" (25cm) (30 links) of natural
    brass 5x7mm etched cable chain
72" (183cm) of gunmetal 20-gauge
    wire
120" (305cm) of gunmetal 24-gauge
    wire
3½" (9cm) of purple ³⁄₈" (1cm) emBead
    silk cording

TOOLS

Bead stop
Wire cutters
Chain-nose pliers
Flat-nose pliers
Round-nose pliers
Nylon-jaw pliers

FINISHED SIZE

19" (48cm)

A glass beetle, handmade by Margaret Zinser, inspired this botanic beauty. Attached to silk cording with loosely wrapped wire, leaves made of pressed glass and natural brass become the perfect environment for this beetle to climb. With such a powerful centerpiece, only small amounts of color interspersed in brass chain are needed to complete this stunning necklace.

1   Use 12" (31cm) of 20-gauge wire to string 1 brass rondelle. Place a bead stop 4½" (11cm) from the end of the wire. Gently pass the wire through the silk cording. String 1 brass rondelle. Tuck the brass rondelles into the ends of the silk cording.

2   Use one end of the wire to form a wrapped loop, coiling the wire around the end of the silk cording and hiding its raw edge. Remove the bead stop and repeat with the other end of the wire.

3   Fold 12" (31cm) of 20-gauge wire in half using chain-nose pliers. Use round-nose pliers to grip the wire at the fold and make one and one-half coils.

4   Use both ends of wire to string the beetle bead. Use one of the wire ends to coil around the other end of the wire up away from the beetle bead for about ⅓" (.84cm), then coiling back toward the bead. Use the other end of the wire to form a wrapped loop around the center of the silk cording; wrap the wire around the silk cording three more times, then coil the wire end down toward the beetle.

Imitation pearls were developed in France in the seventeenth century. Essence d'orient (ground iridescent fish scales mixed with lacquer to resemble nacre) was placed inside small hollow glass beads, with wax added to the center of the beads for weight. Today, the best imitation pearls are still made this way. Less expensive imitation pearls are simply dipped and coated with a substance not much changed from the original formula for Essence d'orient.

5 Tuck the end of 60" (152cm) of 24-gauge wire under the wire wraps around the center of the silk cording. Wrap the wire around the silk cording three times, ending with the wire coming up from the bottom of the silk cording.

6 String 1 fire-polished round. Push the bead down so that it is on top of the silk cording. Wrap the wire around the silk three times.

7 String 1 pressed-glass leaf. Hold the leaf at the bottom of the silk cording and wrap the wire around the silk three times.

8 Repeat Step 6.

9 Repeat Step 7, holding the leaf at the top of the silk cording.

10 Repeat Step 6.

11 String 1 brass leaf and 1 pressed-glass leaf. Hold the leaves at the bottom of the silk cording and wrap the wire around the silk three times.

12 Repeat Step 6. Repeat Step 9. Repeat Step 6. Repeat Step 7.

13 Wrap the wire around the silk cording until you reach the brass rondelle. Wrap the wire back toward the center, wrapping over the previous wraps. Hide the end of the wire beneath the center wires.

14 Repeat Steps 5–13 on the other side of the beetle bead.

15 Use chain- and flat-nose pliers to open and close links of the chain to divide the chain into ten 3-link pieces.

16 Attach the end of one piece of chain to one of the wrapped loops of the centerpiece.

17 Use 3" (8cm) of 20-gauge wire to form a wrapped loop that attaches to the other end of the chain. String 1 brass rondelle, 1 lampworked glass rondelle, and 1 brass rondelle. Form a wrapped loop that attaches to one piece of chain.

18 Use 3" (8cm) of 20-gauge wire to form a wrapped loop that attaches to the other end of the chain. String 1 fire-polished round, 1 brass rondelle, and 1 fire-polished round. Form a wrapped loop that attaches to one piece of chain.

19 Repeat Step 17. Repeat Step 18.

20 Repeat Steps 16–19 for the other half of the necklace. Open the final link of chain on one half of the necklace and attach it to the lobster clasp.

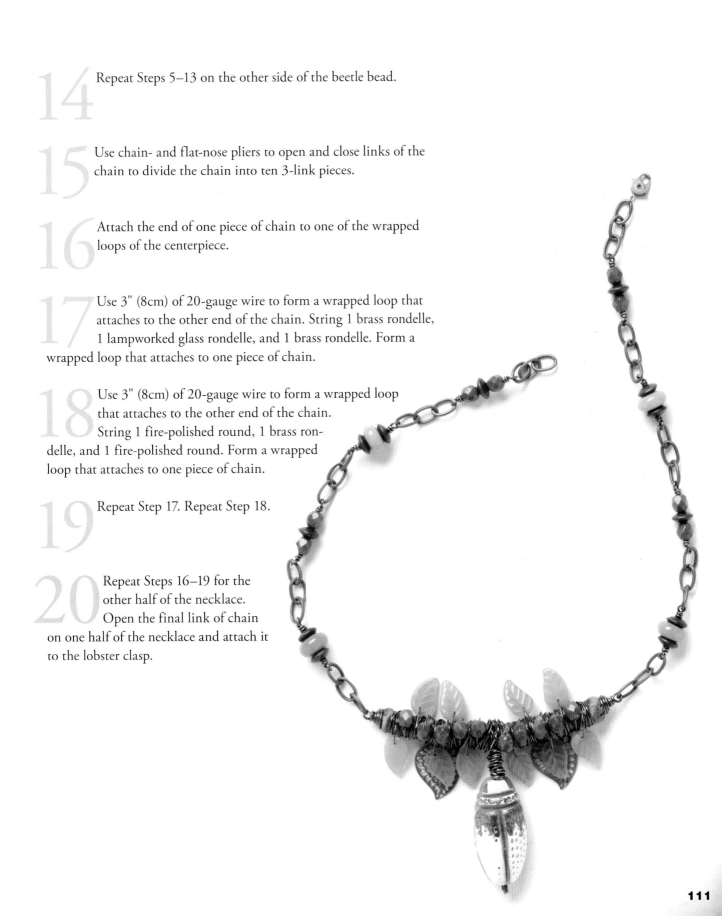

Techniques and Findings

Cones

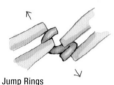

Jump Rings

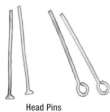

Head Pins

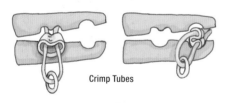

Wrapped Bails

Dangles

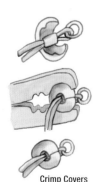

Crimp Tubes

Crimp Covers

Cones, Dangles, and Wrapped Bails

Cones

Use cones to finish a multistrand piece. Attach each strand of beads to a wrapped loop or an eye pin. Use the wrapped-loop wire to string the wide end of a cone, covering the ends of the stringing material. Form a wrapped loop at the tip of the cone that attaches to a clasp.

Dangles

Dangles can be strung as they are, attached using jump rings, or linked onto other loops. Use a head pin or eye pin to string the bead(s), then form a simple or wrapped loop.

Jump Rings

Jump rings connect holes and loops. Open a jump ring by grasping each side of its opening with a pair of pliers. Don't pull apart. Instead, twist in opposite directions so that you can open and close without distorting the shape.

Head Pins

Head pins are straight wires with a ball or flat disc at one end. Eye pins are straight wires that end in a simple loop.

Wrapped Bails

Wrapped bails turn side-drilled beads, usually teardrops, into pendants. Center the bead on a 6" (15 cm) piece of wire. Bend both ends of the wire up the sides and across the top of the bead. Bend one end straight up at the center of the bead and wrap the other wire around it to form a few coils. Form a wrapped loop with the straight-up wire, wrapping it back down over the already-formed coils. Trim the excess wire.

Crimping

Crimp tubes are seamless tubes of metal that come in several sizes. To use, string a crimp tube through the connection finding. Pass back through the tube, leaving a short tail. Use the back notch of the crimping pliers to press the length of the tube down between the wires, enclosing them in separate chambers of the crescent shape. Rotate the tube 90° and use the front notch of the pliers to fold the two chambers onto themselves, forming a clean cylinder. Trim the excess wire.

Crimp ends/leather crimps have a loop attached to a large crimp tube. Place one on the end of beading wire or a leather cord, then use pliers to flatten it. For added security, dab leather with glue before placing it in the crimp.

Crimp covers hide a 2mm crimp tube and give a professional finish. To attach, gently hold a crimp cover in the front notch of the crimping pliers. Insert the crimped tube and gently squeeze the pliers, encasing the tube inside the cover.

Twisted crimps are crimp tubes that have been "twisted," creating ridges on the inside of the tube that grip beading wire. Crimp beads are serrated metal beads. Twisted crimps and crimp beads can be secured by squeezing them flat with chain- or flat-nose pliers.

Twsted Crimp

Finishing and Starting New Threads

Tie off your old thread when it's about 4" (10cm) long by making a simple knot between beads. Pass through a few beads and pull tight to hide the knot. Weave through a few more beads and trim the thread close to the work. Start the new thread by tying a knot between beads and weaving through a few beads. Pull tight to hide the knot. Weave through several beads until you reach the place to resume beading.

Half-hitch Knot

Knots
Half-Hitch Knot

Half-hitch knots may be worked with two or more strands—one strand is knotted over one or more other strands. Form a loop around the cord(s). Pull the end through the loop just formed and pull tight. Repeat for the length of cord you want to cover.

Lark's Head Knot

Lark's head knots are great for securing stringing material to another piece, such as a ring or a donut. Begin by folding the stringing material in half. Pass the fold through a ring or donut. Pull the ends through the loop created and pull tight.

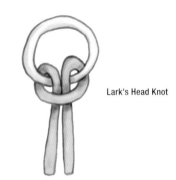

Lark's Head Knot

Square Knot

The square knot is the classic sturdy knot for securing most stringing materials. First make an overhand knot, passing the right end over the left end. Next, make another overhand knot, this time passing the left end over the right end. Pull tight.

Square Knot

Surgeon's Knot

The surgeon's knot is very secure and therefore good for finishing off most stringing materials. Tie an overhand knot, right over left, but instead of one twist over the left cord, make at least two. Tie another overhand knot, left over right, and pull tight.

Overhand Knot

The overhand knot is the basic knot for tying off thread. Make a loop with the stringing material. Pass the cord that lies behind the loop over the front cord and through the loop. Pull tight.

Surgeon's Knot

Pass Through vs Pass Back Through

Pass through means to move your needle in the same direction that the beads have been strung. Pass back through means to move your needle in the opposite direction.

Overhand Knot

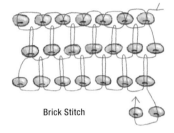

Brick Stitch

Brick-stitch Decrease

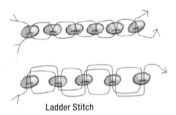

Ladder Stitch

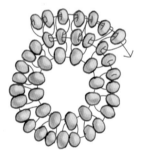

Circular Square Stitch

Flat One-drop Peyote Stitch

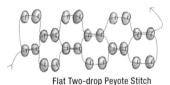

Flat Two-drop Peyote Stitch

Stitches

Brick Stitch

Begin by creating a foundation row in ladder stitch or using a secured thread. String 2 beads and pass under the closest exposed loop of the foundation row and back through the second bead. String 1 bead and pass under the next exposed loop and back through the bead just strung; repeat.

To decrease within a row, string 1 bead and skip a loop of thread on the previous row, passing under the second loop and back through the bead.
To increase within a row, work two stitches in the same loop on the previous row.

Ladder Stitch

Using two needles, one threaded on each end of the thread, pass one needle through 1 or more beads from left to right and pass the other needle through the same beads from right to left. Continue adding beads by crisscrossing both needles through 1 bead at a time. Use this stitch to make strings of beads or as the foundation for brick stitch.

For a single-needle ladder, string 2 beads and pass through them again. String 1 bead. Pass through the last stitched bead and the one just strung. Repeat, adding 1 bead at a time and working in a figure-eight pattern.

Circular Square Stitch

String the first round of beads and pass through them again to form a circle. Start a new round by stringing 2 beads; pass through the last bead of the first round and through the 2 beads just strung. Repeat all around, passing through the next bead of the previous round for each 2 new beads strung. At the end of the round, pass through the whole round again to tighten the beads. Start a new round by stringing 2 beads; pass through the last bead of the first round and through the 2 beads just strung. String 1 bead and pass through the next bead of the previous round and the bead just strung. Repeat around, stitching 1 or 2 beads to each bead of the previous round, adjusting the count as necessary to keep the work flat.

Flat Peyote Stitch

One-drop peyote stitch begins by stringing an even number of beads to create the first two rows. Begin the third row by stringing 1 bead and passing through the second-to-last bead of the previous rows. String another bead and pass through the fourth-to-last bead of the previous rows. Continue adding 1 bead at a time, passing over every other bead of the previous rows.

Two-drop peyote stitch is worked the same as above, but with 2 beads at a time instead of 1.

To make a mid-project decrease, simply pass thread through 2 beads without adding a bead in the "gap." In the next row, work a regular one-drop peyote over the decrease. Keep tension taut to avoid holes.

To make a mid-project increase, work a two-drop over a one-drop in one row. In the next row, work a one-drop peyote between the two-drop. For a smooth increase, use very narrow beads for both the two-drop and the one-drop between.

Square Stitch
Begin by stringing a row of beads. For the second row, string 2 beads, pass through the second-to-last bead of the first row, and back through the second bead of those just strung. Continue by stringing 1 bead, passing through the third-to-last bead of the first row, and back through the bead just strung. Repeat this looping technique to the end of the row.

To make a decrease, weave thread through the previous row and exit from the bead adjacent to the place you want to decrease. Continue working in square stitch.

To make an increase, string the number of beads at the end of the row you want to increase. Work the next row the same as the previous row.

Tubular Herringbone Stitch
Begin with a foundation row of ladder stitch. Join the ends together to form a tube. String 2 beads. Pass down through the next bead and up through the bead after it. Repeat around the tube. At the end of the round, pass through the first beads of the previous and current rounds to step up to the new round.

Stringing
Stringing is a technique in which you use a beading wire, needle and thread, or other material to gather beads into a strand.

Tension Bead
String a bead larger than those you are working with, then pass through the bead one or more times, making sure not to split your thread. The bead will be able to slide along but will still provide tension to work against when you're beading the first two rows.

Wireworking
To form a simple loop, use flat-nose pliers to make a 90° bend at least ⅜" (1cm) from the end of the wire. Use round-nose pliers to grasp the wire after the bend; roll the pliers toward the bend, but not past it, to preserve the 90° bend. Use your thumb to continue the wrap around the nose of the pliers. Trim the wire next to the bend. Open a simple loop by grasping each side of its opening with a pair of pliers. Don't pull apart. Instead, twist in opposite directions so that you can open and close without distorting the shape.

To form a wrapped loop, begin with a 90° bend at least 2" (5cm) from the end of the wire. Use round-nose pliers to form a simple loop with a tail overlapping the bend. Wrap the tail tightly down the neck of the wire to create a couple of coils. Trim the excess wire to finish. Make a thicker, heavier-looking wrapped loop by wrapping the wire back up over the coils, toward the loop, and trimming at the loop.

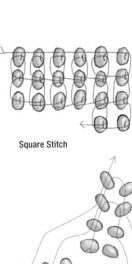

Square Stitch

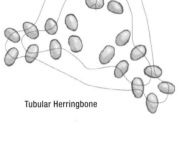

Tubular Herringbone

Stringing

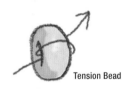

Tension Bead

Simple Loop

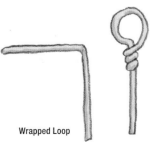

Wrapped Loop

RESOURCES

Materials

Africa Calls, 20
African trade beads: Africa Direct
Millefiori rounds: Bella Venetian Beads
Clasp: Shiana
FireLine braided beading thread and beading needles: Fusionbeads.com

Autumn Heart, 42
Lampworked glass heart: Brent Graber
Czech pressed-glass beads: Bokamo Designs
Seed beads: Jane's Fiber and Beads
Chain, clasp, wire, and findings: Fusionbeads.com

Bollywood in Blue, 48
Lampworked beads: Bokamo Designs
1.5mm glass cubes, vermeil filigree, and gold beads and findings: Fusionbeads.com
Size 8° seed beads: Bead Cache

Bright Amulet, 78
Javanese lampworked glass beads: The Bead Goes On
Venetian lampworked mosaic squares: VenetianBeadShop.com
Seed beads: Jane's Fiber and Beads
Clasp: Jess Imports
Paisley charms, FireLine braided beading thread, and findings: Fusionbeads.com
Beading wire: Soft Flex Company

Come to My Party, 100
Venetian lampworked beads: VenetianBeadShop.com
Czech pressed-glass beads: Raven's Journey
Clasp: Jess Imports
Size 11° seed beads: Beyond Beadery
Size 8° seed beads: Bead Cache

Dharma Wheel, 72
Seed beads: Jane's Fiber and Beads
Czech pressed-glass beads: Raven's Journey
Wood links and FireLine braided beading thread: Fusionbeads.com
Terrifically Tacky Tape: Artbeads.com
Natural brass clasp and jump rings: JamieHogsett.com

Honey Blossoms, 24
Lampworked glass beads: Dyed in the Fire Designs
Seed beads: Beyond Beadery
Natural brass charms, chain, ear wires, and wire: JamieHogsett.com

Le Beau Jardin, 108
Lampworked glass beetle and rondelles: MZglass
Czech pressed-glass beads: Raven's Journey
Silk cord: emBead
Natural brass filigree, chain, beads, and findings: JamieHogsett.com

Lotus Link, 64
Clasp, links, and head pins: Shiana
Jump rings: Via Murano
Seed beads: Jane's Fiber and Beads
Czech pressed-glass beads: Raven's Journey
Javanese lampworked glass beads: The Bead Goes On
Beading wire and findings: Soft Flex Company

My Nest, 26
Czech pressed-glass beads: Raven's Journey
Size 11° seed beads: Beyond Beadery
Size 15° seed beads: Jane's Fiber and Beads
Pewter beads and sterling silver clasp: Green Girl Studios
FireLine braided beading thread: Fusionbeads.com
Beading wire: Soft Flex Company

Ocean Journey, 34
Czech pressed-glass beads: Raven's Journey
Polymer clay round beads: Heather Wynn
Venetian lampworked beads: VenetianBeadShop.com
Javanese lampworked glass beads: The Bead Goes On
African trade beads: Africa Direct
Natural brass beads and findings: JamieHogsett.com
Beading wire: Soft Flex Company

Passionflower, 38
Metal seed beads: Beyond Beadery
Lampworked glass flowers: Fusionbeads.com
Brass filigree, bead caps, jump rings, and clasp: JamieHogsett.com
Czech pressed-glass beads: Raven's Journey
Glass rings: Michaels
Beading wire: Soft Flex Company

Radiant Bloom, 58
Magatamas, cubes, seed beads, and Nymo thread: Fusionbeads.com
Natural brass clasp, chain, and findings: JamieHogsett.com

Rhumba, 104
Lampworked glass beads: Z-beads
Seed beads: Beyond Beadery
Clasp: Fire Mountain Gems and Beads
Beading wire and findings: Soft Flex Company

Romancing the Acorn, 84
Lampworked glass acorn and stamped beads: Joyce Rooks
Venetian lampworked round beads and clasp: Via Murano
Seed and twist bugle beads: Jane's Fiber and Beads
Components, wire, and findings: Fusionbeads.com
Beading wire: Soft Flex Company

Starflowers, 52
Czech pressed-glass daggers and fire-polished beads: Raven's Journey
Size 11° seed beads: Jane's Fiber and Beads
Size 8° seed beads: Beyond Beadery
Jump rings: Via Murano
Clasp, wire, and FireLine braided beading thread: Fusionbeads.com

Sweet Treat, 88
Venetian-glass curved tubes: Via Murano
Black silver clasp, charms, beads, and findings: Shiana
Seed beads: Beyond Beadery
Czech pressed-glass beads: Raven's Journey

Tribal Relics, 96
Czech pressed-glass tubes, clasp, and cord ends: Bokamo Designs
Other Czech pressed-glass beads: Raven's Journey
Size 8° seed beads: Beyond Beadery
Size 11° seed beads: Jane's Fiber and Beads
Leather cord: Artbeads.com
8mm jump ring: Via Murano
Other jump rings, wire, and findings: Fusionbeads.com
Beading wire: Soft Flex Company

Venetian Vines, 68
Czech fire-polished beads: Artbeads.com
Venetian-glass textured frit beads: VenetianBeadShop.com
Venetian bicolor foil discs: Bella Venetian Beads
Leaf connectors, clasp, wire, and findings: Fusionbeads.com
Beading wire: Soft Flex Company

Wonder Woman, 92
Chevrons: Bella Venetian Beads
Seed beads: Jane's Fiber and Beads
All other materials: Fusionbeads.com

Sources

Africa Direct
2300 Krameria St.
Denver, CO 80207
(303) 316-7570
eliza500@aol.com
africadirect.com

Artbeads.com
11901 137th Ave. Ct. KPN, Unit 100
Gig Harbor, WA 98329
(253) 857-2372
artbeads.com

Bead Cache
3307 S. College Ave. #105
Fort Collins, CO 80525
(970) 224-4322

The Bead Goes On
14 Church St.
PO Box 592
Vineyard Haven, MA 02568
(866) 861-2323
beadgoeson.com

Bella Venetian Beads
424 Fort Hill Dr., Ste. 102
Naperville, IL 60540
(630) 305-8232
bellavenetianbeads.com

Beyond Beadery
PO Box 460
Rollinsville, CO 80474
(800) 840-5548
beyondbeadery.com

Bokamo Designs
5609 W. 99th St.
Overland Park, KS 66207
(913) 648-4296
bokamodesigns.com

Brent Graber
"Mr. Smiley"
(407) 383-4596
brentgraber.com

Dyed in the Fire Designs
Patti Cahill
PO Box 1659
Mars Hill, NC 28754
(828) 689-8934
plcahill@madison.main.nc.us

emBead
2675 W. Grand Ave., Ste. 501
Chicago, IL 60612
(773) 227-2524
info@embead.com
embead.com

Fire Mountain Gems and Beads
1 Fire Mountain Wy.
Grants Pass, OR 97526-2373
(800) 355-2137
firemountaingems.com

Fusionbeads.com
13024 Stone Wy. N.
Seattle, WA 98133
(888) 781-3559
fusionbeads.com

Green Girl Studios
PO Box 19389
Asheville, NC 28815
(828) 298-2263
greengirlstudios@gmail.com
greengirlstudios.com

Heather Wynn
heatherwynn.com

Jamie Hogsett
jamiehogsett.com

Jane's Fiber and Beads
5415 Andrew Johnson Hwy. E.
PO Box 110
Afton, TN 37616
(888) 497-2665
janesfiberandbeads.com

Jess Imports
66 Gough St.
San Francisco, CA 94102
(415) 626-1433
jessimports.com

Joyce Rooks
(760) 492-3805
joycerooks.com

MZglass
Margaret Zinser
(520) 798-1609
mzglass.com

Michaels
michaels.com

Raven's Journey
PO Box 3099
Port Angeles, WA 98362
(206) 406-7491
theravenstore.com

Shiana
Pam Thien
PO Box 22
Seacon Sq. Post Office
Bangkok, Thailand, UT 10254
shiana.com

Soft Flex Company
PO Box 80
Sonoma, CA 95476
(866) 925-FLEX (3539)
softflexcompany.com

VenetianBeadShop.com
1008 Stewart Dr.
Sunnyvale, CA 94085
(800) 439-3551
venetianbeadshop.com

Via Murano
17654 Newhope St., Ste. A
Fountain Valley, CA 92708
(877) 842-6872
viamurano.com

Z-Beads
Sarah Moran
z-beads.com

RELATED READING

For more beading designs and techniques, join the community at beadingdaily.com, where life meets beading, or subscribe to Interweave's beading magazines:

Beadwork
Step by Step Beads
Step by Step Wire Jewelry
Stringing

Books

Dubin, Lois Sherr. *The History of Beads, from 30,000 B.C. to the Present*. New York: Harry N. Abrams, 1987.

Mann, Elise. *The Bead Directory: The Complete Guide to Choosing and Using More Than 600 Beautiful Beads*. Loveland, Colorado: Interweave, 2006.

Miller, Judith. *Collector's Guides: Costume Jewelry*. New York: DK Publishing, 2003.

Murray, Maureen. *All About Beads: A Guide to Beads and Bead Jewellery Making*. London: B. T. Batsford, 1995.

Sersich, Stephanie. *Designing Jewelry with Glass Beads*. Loveland, Colorado: Interweave, 2008.

Websites

Dale Chihuly. chihuly.com. (The world-renowned glass artist is one of the premier initiators of the American Studio Glass Movement. He was a co-founder of the Pilchuck Glass School in the Pacific Northwest in 1971.)

Corning Museum of Glass. cmog.org. (Located in Corning, New York, and founded by the glass manufacturer of the same name, the museum's website has extensive resource information on glassmaking and glass artifacts, historical and contemporary.)

Museum of Glass. museumofglass.org. (The Northwest institution in Tacoma, Washington, offers glassmaking classes and glass exhibits.)

Pilchuck Glass School. pilchuck.com. (This is the most prominent glassmaking school in the country, offering studio training in the art.)

INDEX

Create Beautiful Jewelry

with these inspiring resources from Interweave

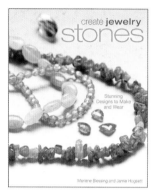

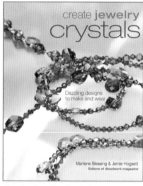